S·H·P

THE
SCHOOLS
HISTORY
PROJECT

DISCOVERING THE PAST Y8

SOCIETIES IN CHANGE

TEACHERS' RESOURCE BOOK

JOHN MURRAY

Pupils' Book ISBN 0–7195–4975–2
Teachers' Resource Book ISBN 0–7195–4976–0

© Colin Shephard, Chris Hinton, John Hite, Tim Lomas, 1992

First published 1992
by John Murray (Publishers) Ltd
50 Albemarle Street
London W1X 4BD

Illustrations by David Anstey, Art Construction, Peter Bull Art Studio, John Townson/Creation.
Tables by Taurus Graphics

Typeset by Wearset, Boldon, Tyne and Wear
Printed in Great Britain by St Edmundsbury Press, Bury St Edmunds.

A CIP catalogue record for this book is available from the British Library

ISBN 0–7195–4976–0

Contents

Introduction

Discovering the Past

Series Editor
Colin Shephard (Director, Schools History Project)

Series consultants
Tim Lomas (NC History Working Group)
Andy Reid (NCC History Task Group)

Discovering the Past is SHP's integrated series of full-colour course books and teachers' materials for NC History – for all Key Stages.

■ Coherence in Key Stages 3 and 4
The core texts combine core units and SHP-designed supplementary units into a coherent course for each year. In Y8, for instance, the core text examines the dynamics of change in two different periods, in two different societies – the UK 1500–1750 and France 1700–1818. Alternative supplementary study units, such as *The Changing Role of Men and Women*, allow schools to follow a range of pathways without losing that coherence.

■ An issue-based approach
Issues and questions raised by the content give each unit its identity. These genuine historical issues and controversies encourage pupils to question conventional interpretations of the past.

■ The role of the individual
By focusing on case studies of particular places and individuals, the series avoids historical stereotypes. Instead, pupils can begin to appreciate the variety and complexity of a period.

■ Classroom appeal
The series uses the best classroom practices, combining innovation and familiar techniques to ensure variety for the pupil and the teacher. A range of readers, advisers and (in Key Stages 1 and 2) trialling schools have ensured the classroom appeal of the material across the Key Stages.

■ Language control
Language has been carefully monitored to ensure it is appropriate to the age group. This is particularly crucial in Key Stages 1 and 2.

■ Source-based activities
The pupil tasks and enquiries use a wide range of source material – so that work towards AT3 is thoroughly integrated into work towards ATs 1 and 2.

■ Cultural and gender balance
For each year in Key Stage 3 the series provides a non-European unit, to extend the core in an ethnically sensitive manner. For example, in Y7, the Crusades are viewed through both Islamic and Western eyes. The series also covers the roles and experiences of both women and men.

■ Assessment and the Attainment Targets
Enquiry-based pupil tasks and questions are provided throughout to help pupils of all abilities progress through the ATs. Each enquiry has a particular emphasis, but *Discovering the Past* avoids artificially separating work towards the three ATs.

The series is built on SHP's considerable assessment expertise. Guidance on teacher-based assessment is provided. Guidance in preparing pupils for History SATs at fourteen and sixteen will be included in the core texts for Y9 and Y11.

THE SCHOOLS HISTORY PROJECT

This project was set up by the Schools Council in 1972. Its main aim was to suggest suitable alternatives for History teachers, and to promote the use of appropriate materials and teaching methods for their realisation. This involved a reconsideration of the nature of History and its relevance in secondary schools, the design of a syllabus framework which shows the uses of History in the teaching of adolescents, and the setting up of appropriate examinations.

Since 1978 the project has been based at Trinity and All Saints' College, Leeds, where it is one of three curriculum development projects run and supported by the Centre for History Education. The project is now self funding and with the advent of the National Curriculum it has expanded its publications to provide courses throughout the Key Stages for pupils aged five to sixteen. The project provides INSET for all aspects of National Curriculum History.

Enquiries about the project and INSET should be addressed to the Schools History Project, Trinity and All Saints' College, Brownberrie Lane, Horsforth, Leeds LS18 5HD.

Enquiries about the *Discovering the Past* series should be addressed to the publishers, John Murray.

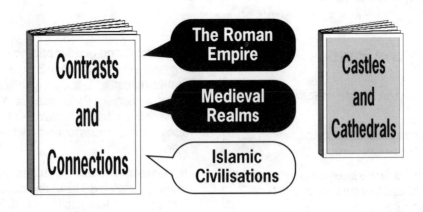

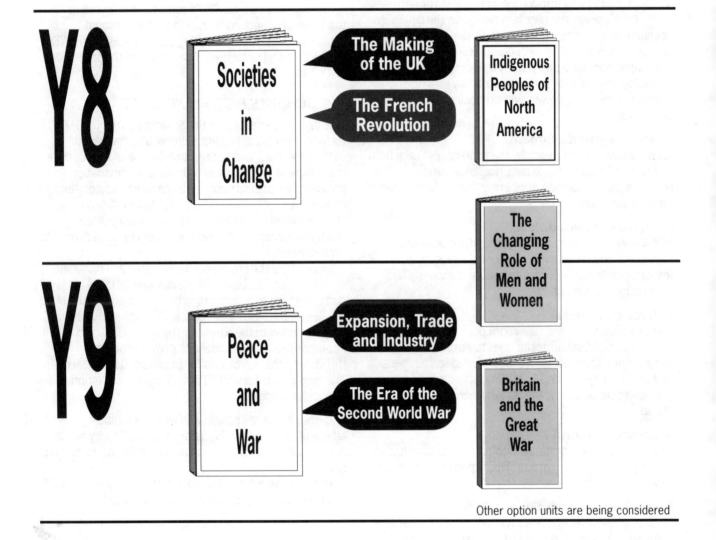

Other option units are being considered

CHOOSING A PATHWAY FOR KEY STAGE 3

The series offers you different pathways through Key Stage 3. Four possible pathways are shown opposite. Each of them can be resourced from the core texts plus optional units. There are a number of other possible pathways.

The scheme gives you the opportunity to vary your course from year to year, or for individual members of a department to choose different pathways, still using the same book stock. So changing your course in future years will not mean changing all your books – a great benefit in times of funding uncertainty. Flexibility is further ensured by provision for schools to conceive and design their own study units.

THE PATHWAYS

	PATHWAY 1	*PATHWAY 2*	*PATHWAY 3*	*PATHWAY 4*
Y7				
a bridging unit between Key Stages 2 and 3	The Roman Empire	The Roman Empire	The Roman Empire	The Roman Empire
including optional local work from Castles and Cathedrals	Medieval Realms	Medieval Realms	Medieval Realms	Medieval Realms
	Islamic Civilisations	Islamic Civilisations	Castles and Cathedrals	
Y8				
comparative work on revolution and change	The Making of the UK	The Making of the UK	The Making of the UK	The Making of the UK
	The French Revolution	The French Revolution	The French Revolution	The French Revolution
a school designed study unit	Local history linked to The Making of the UK or to Expansion, Trade and Industry	The Changing Role of Men and Women, or Britain and the Great War	Indigenous Peoples of North America	Indigenous Peoples of North America
Y9				
preparation for SATs at the end of Key Stage 3	Expansion, Trade and Industry	Expansion, Trade and Industry	Expansion, Trade and Industry	Expansion, Trade and Industry
	The Era of the Second World War	The Era of the Second World War	The Era of the Second World War	Britain and The Great War
				The Era of the Second World War

KEY:

Core		Category B	A European Turning Point HSU
Category A	A British HSU	Category C	A Past Non-European Society HSU

Societies in Change

AIMS

■ The main aim of this course is to help pupils realise how fascinating History can be. The course is founded on the belief that twelve- and thirteen-year-olds can cope with an investigation of real historical issues – issues that would interest a historian – if they are presented at an appropriate level.

■ The Programme of Study for **The Making of the UK** has been covered. This has been done through the use of enquiries, rather than by slavishly following the list of topics in the Programme of Study. For example, there is no separate section on religious differences. Instead, this subject is tackled through enquiries on entertainments, the Reformation, the Gunpowder Plot and the Glorious Revolution. The table opposite shows how the content of the core unit has been covered.

■ Many of the topics in units such as **The Making of the UK** are difficult ones for Y8 pupils to grasp. We have taken the view that the best way to allow pupils to develop an understanding of events such as the Reformation and the Civil War is through the study of particular people, places and events rather than by trying to tell the whole story in a superficial and general way. Thus the work on the Reformation focuses on changes to a church in a Suffolk village, and on the roles and beliefs of Henry VIII and Mary. The work on what life was like in the Civil War concentrates on the experiences of Lady Harley defending Brampton Castle. The work on the political union of the United Kingdom focuses on an investigation of the Jacobite Rebellion of 1745, asking whether this showed Scottish dissatisfaction with the union.

■ The two units in this book – The Making of the UK and The French Revolution – build on each other to make up a coherent scheme of work for Y8. They should be seen as a whole.

Some issues are consciously tackled in a comparative way across the two units: for example, the trials and executions of the two kings, Charles I of England and Louis XVI of France. On other occasions the comparisons are left implicit and picked up in this Teachers' Resource Book so that comparative work can be undertaken if desired. For example, there are worksheets comparing the causes of the English and French Revolutions, comparing the significance of the two revolutions and comparing Cromwell and Napoleon.

The aim is that by the end of Y8 pupils should appreciate the dynamics of various kinds of historical change. They should see the causes of religious, social, political and economic changes in two societies. They will also see the impact these changes had on ordinary people.

■ You will see from the matrix on page 14 that the Attainment Targets, including virtually every Statement of Attainment, are covered by this course. However, it has been neither assessment led nor AT led. Rather, the aim has been to provide questions and activities that are worthwhile in their own right and create learning opportunities for the pupils. The majority of these questions and activities are to be used simply to give pupils access to the ATs, rather than for assessment purposes.

Furthermore, the aim has been to design the questions and activities to be genuinely accessible by all abilities. We have allowed for differentiation by outcome rather than by task, while using the detailed notes and worksheets in the teachers' book to highlight occasions when support may be necessary for some pupils. There is further guidance on this subject on page 8.

■ Finally, we have aimed to help pupils to learn how to do the work of the historian; to organise their historical ideas and findings, to ask their own questions, to collect and record information, and to present their results using a range of different techniques.

The book is based on issues and enquiries in order to encourage pupils to reach their own conclusions and to question stereotypical views of the past. Care has been taken to provide information about each enquiry in sufficient depth to allow pupils to base their conclusions on full and sound evidence.

It is very important that pupils produce some history of their own, and construct their own view of the past. The major activities at the end of each enquiry throughout the book are geared to this fundamental objective.

The making of the United Kingdom: Crowns, Parliaments and peoples 1500 to 1750

Pupils should be taught the major political, social and religious changes which shaped the history of Britain during this period. The main focus should be on two themes: the political unification of Britain, and the changing relationships between Crown, Parliament and people.

Pupils should be taught about:

The political unification of Britain
- the formation of the United Kingdom, including the Acts of Union of 1536 and 1543 (Wales) and the Treaty of 1707 (Scotland), and the changing relationship between England and Ireland

The power of the monarchy and its relationship with Parliament and people
- the functions and importance of the Crown
- the changing relationships of Crown, Parliament and people in the era of the Civil War and Interregnum (1639 to 1660) and Glorious Revolution (1688)

Changes in ideas and the arts
- the impact on the arts and architecture of political and religious change
- the scientific revolution of the seventeenth century

The diversity of British society
- social classes in early modern Britain
- religious differences and relations between Roman Catholics, Anglicans and Nonconformists
- regional differences in wealth, lifestyle, religion and culture

Column key (left to right):
1. religious differences and relations between Roman Catholics, Anglicans and Nonconformists
2. regional differences in wealth, lifestyle, religion and culture
3. social classes in early modern Britain
4. the scientific revolution of the seventeenth century
5. the impact on the arts and architecture of political and religious change
6. the changing relationships of Crown, Parliament and people
7. the functions and importance of the Crown
8. the formation of the United Kingdom

Topic	1	2	3	4	5	6	7	8
England in the 1500s		✓	✓					
Were the poor really poor?		✓	✓					
Were the rich really rich?			✓					
Private lives			✓	✓				
Could you enjoy yourself?	✓		✓	✓				
Was the Catholic Church still healthy in 1500?	✓							
Henry VIII: Catholic or Protestant?	✓						✓	✓
Bloody Queen Mary?	✓						✓	
The Reformation in English villages	✓	✓				✓		
Were the Catholics framed?	✓							
What did Elizabeth look like?					✓	✓	✓	
Why did Civil War break out in 1642?	✓					✓	✓	✓
Who fought whom?						✓		✓
What was life like during the Civil War?		✓				✓		
Why did the Royalists lose at Marston Moor?						✓		
Why did the English execute their king?						✓	✓	
Charles the martyr or Charles the traitor?					✓	✓	✓	
What kind of man was Oliver Cromwell?						✓	✓	✓
The world turned upside down			✓					
James II: the same old story?	✓					✓	✓	✓
Uniting the Kingdom						✓	✓	✓
How united was the United Kingdom?		✓	✓				✓	
Science and superstition		✓		✓				
How did London change?		✓		✓				
A tour around Britain		✓	✓	✓				

SOCIETIES IN CHANGE

ORGANISING THE Y8 COURSE

The two units

We are assuming that most schools will give approximately a term's teaching time to each unit. Each unit has a separate set of notes in this book, but links between the units are picked up as they arise.

Each unit of the pupils' book is split into a number of *enquiries*. The enquiry is a discrete piece of work on a discrete theme. Each enquiry covers one, two, three or four double-page spreads in the pupils' book.

There is usually enough in an enquiry to keep a class busy for one or two weeks, with or without homework. However, schools spend such varying amounts of time on History that we have had to build in a great deal of flexibility. There is obviously too much material in each of the units to complete everything in one term. This is deliberate, and is intended to give teachers scope to choose their own pathways through each unit, deciding which enquiries to concentrate on and which to leave out.

It is possible in The Making of the UK to select a limited number of enquiries and still to cover the contents of the Programme of Study. For example, you might choose:

Were the poor really poor?
Were the rich really rich?
Henry VIII: Catholic or Protestant?
Bloody Queen Mary?
Why did civil war break out in 1642?
What was life like during the Civil War?
What kind of man was Oliver Cromwell?
James II – the same old story?
Uniting the Kingdom
How united was the United Kingdom?
Science and superstition
How did London change?

This selection of enquiries covers all elements of the Programme of Study. Some elements are covered in more depth than others, but this is deliberate.

You could make a different selection. Indeed, you could use different enquiries from one year to the next. However, any selection would need to include enquiries on the Civil War and the Making of the United Kingdom, as these form the backbone of the Programme of Study. The Programme of Study matrix (page 5) will help you.

If you make your own selection of enquiries you should also check with the matrix on page 14 that it provides a reasonably even coverage of the ATs. In practice this will not be a problem, as the majority of the enquiries in this book, even though they focus on one strand of the ATs, do also access the other strands.

On occasions you might wish to use different enquiries with different members of the class. The class should then be split into separate study groups for a couple of weeks. For example, in The Making of the UK, three separate groups could look at the poor (pages 6–11), the rich (pages 12–15) and entertainment (pages 22–25). Each group should make a presentation to the rest of the class at the end of their two- or three-week project. More importantly, they can also select what they regard as the two or three most important tasks from their enquiry for the rest of the class to tackle.

Within an enquiry there are similar opportunities for choice. For example, in The Making of the UK pupils could be split into study groups for the enquiry *Private lives*, one group to look at each of *Getting married*, *Being married* and *Having children*. In The French Revolution separate study groups could be formed for the enquiry *Did French people support the Revolution?*, one group to focus on *The sans-culottes*, one on *The counter-revolutionaries* and a third on *The murder of Marat*.

These are a few examples of how we have aimed, wherever possible, to involve pupils fully in the choices governing what they learn and how they learn. Listening to pupils' own questions, offering a choice of task and allowing them to pursue their own favoured line of enquiry will all help increase motivation.

Each enquiry contains questions and activities to be done en route. These appear in yellow boxes. For convenience, the questions normally return to number 1 after a new sub-heading.

At the end of the enquiry, in a blue box, there is usually a major piece of work bringing together themes from the previous few spreads. The questions and discussions during the rest of the enquiry are an important part of the process of getting ready to answer these summary questions.

The main purpose of the summary questions is to show how pupils have brought together the skills from the various Attainment Targets. However, they are also crucial for harnessing pupil motivation. Pupils like to have something to show for the work they have done in History, and the summary questions and activities are designed to achieve this.

The enquiry is also the basis for the organisation of the detailed teaching notes which begin on page 23 of this book. For each enquiry there is:

■ a brief description or statement of purpose
■ boxes summarising which of the Statements of Attainment are most likely to be accessed by each set of questions
■ guidance on how to introduce a topic, additional background information for teachers, suggestions on which questions to use for discussion and which for written work, and ideas for support or extension work – including links to photocopiable worksheets, suggested resource books, etc.
■ some detail on the thinking that has gone into the design of the questions, so that it can be clear how the Attainment Targets are working in practice.

For each unit there are also a number of photocopiable worksheets. These provide support and extension material. Some of them are designed to be suitable for homework where it is impossible for pupils to use the pupils' books.

Questions and activities

There are hundreds of questions in this book. Needless to say, they are not all intended for written work. The questions in the yellow boxes are often best used for class discussion. They are there to help pupils interrogate sources and to approach very gradually the issue which is posed in the enquiry. They are like stepping stones towards the summary question at the end of the enquiry. So all the questions should be addressed in class or group discussion in some way, because they are designed either to introduce or to reinforce new ideas, skills and concepts. It may well be that pupils are asked to give a written response to only one question in four. We have made it clear in the detailed notes that follow when an exercise is particularly appropriate for oral work (e.g. page 22 of The Making of the UK) or for written work (e.g. page 69 of The Making of the UK). Other questions require pupils to role-play, match, prioritise, etc. A wide range of learning techniques is used throughout.

Where a written response is suggested, there are occasions during the year when pupils should be actively encouraged to use word processors to produce their answers. It is an essential part of historical enquiry and communication to be able to present written conclusions clearly and neatly, to redraft conclusions in the light of new evidence, and to introduce new findings or further corroborating evidence into a written answer. Word processing facilities make this more feasible than before. So on occasions where an enquiry involves a wide range of source material or involves an element of presentation to the rest of the class, encourage pupils to use word processors. If you have DTP software available it will be very useful for activities such as those on pages 15 and 21 of the pupils' book. Other IT applications of History — e.g. databases to handle statistical data, graphics, concept keyboard, timeline software programmes, or historical simulations — can be introduced into the course easily at the teacher's discretion, where they will help serve the overall aim of making History enjoyable and accessible for all pupils.

Timelines

The two units cover a period of over 300 years. At twelve, pupils should be increasingly able to piece together these units into their overall map of the past.

As you begin each unit, it is a good idea to cover the whole of one side of the classroom with a timeline. As you start The French Revolution, in particular, be sure to compare the relatively short timescale of the French Revolution unit with the much longer timescale of The Making of the UK. Which came first? Which is the longer? How much longer? Is there any overlap?

As they progress through each unit, pupils' work can be displayed at an appropriate point on the timeline. Don't put many dates on the main timeline; concentrate instead on the relationships between the elements. Whether the Reformation came before or after the Civil War is much more important than the exact dates when each took place.

In the pupils' book you will find various kinds of timelines to help you. Each unit begins with a 'timeframe' for the unit, which can be referred to as necessary during the unit. There is a more detailed photocopiable version of each timeframe in the worksheets for each unit so that each pupil can have his/her own copy to colour code, annotate and refer to.

Secondly, we have provided mini-timelines, at the top of the page, for some of the crucial events in each unit. This not only helps pupils place new events in relation to others they have already studied, but also reinforces a few key dates required by the NC. Ask pupils to copy the mini-timelines into their exercise books, adding the names of all the events shown. The relationships and the sequence are always more important than the absolute dates, and dates are therefore kept to a minimum.

Thirdly, we have used a range of timeline techniques in the text and activities themselves. There are many ways of presenting a sequence of events and we are attempting to use a wide range of them, so that pupils will be increasingly familiar with these different techniques.

Finally, on a number of occasions pupils are asked to draw their own timelines and display their findings on them, e.g. page 35, changes at Melford Church. This gives the pupils an opportunity to demonstrate their grasp of the chronological shape of each period of history.

Using this material in the classroom

Before starting out on an enquiry always read the questions and activities in the pupils' book and the description and suggestions in this teachers' book. Make sure the pupils know the aims of the enquiry or of any piece of work they are undertaking.

A lot of tasks require group work, some suggest the use of a word processor, many suggest the use of display or presentations. All these have implications for how you organise your classroom.

Sources are an integral part of the book — many spreads consist of almost nothing but sources. They are designed to be used; many of the questions within an enquiry are designed to ensure that pupils read, study and understand the source material provided, acquiring AT3 skills in the process.

Consistent with our aim of providing useful learning experiences for the pupils we have translated, simplified and edited written source material to make it accessible. Make it clear to pupils that spelling and punctuation have been made contemporary. Modern equivalent words have been substituted where necessary, or definitions provided. Major edits have been shown by elipses. However, the sense and meaning of all sources have been preserved.

The source line — which introduces and describes the source being studied — is an important tool for the pupil. It contains the details that pupils will need to know to answer any questions, such as who made or wrote the source and when. Encourage pupils to see these source lines as an important part of the evidence.

Further evidence about some of the sources and some of the writers or artists has been provided in the detailed notes on each unit where it is helpful.

In most questions the reason pupils give for their answers are as important as the answers themselves. In explaining why they have answered in a certain way they will reveal how deeply they have understood an issue. We have not, however, constantly reiterated in the questions 'explain your answer', as it gets highly repetitive. Twelve-year-olds should be aware that all historical answers require backing up by evidence. However, you might want to remind pupils of this more often than we have done.

Differentiation

First-hand classroom experience with Y7 material in the *Discovering the Past* series has made it clear that pupils of all abilities can tackle the type of questions and issues in this book, *provided that they are not overwhelmed by being given too many sources, and that the sources they do use are of a suitable level of difficulty.*

Experience with Y7 shows that one successful approach with mixed ability classes is to have all pupils attempting the same tasks but to reduce the amount of source material for some of them. This can be done in a number of ways. Look, for example, at the Activity on page 27 – writing a report on the state of the English Church in 1500:
- You can divide the class into groups and ask each group to base their report on just one source. The reports of the groups can then be compared.
- Some groups can use just one source and others can use all the sources. This can be quite successfully done if the groups are carefully selected.
- Instead of splitting pupils into groups you can, with careful class management, give individual pupils different amounts of source material to use.

Another example might be in questions 3 and 4 on page 49. Pupils could be given two stages and two triggers on the road to Civil War to choose between.

As soon as it becomes clear that a pupil is finding a task difficult, the amount of material he/she is asked to use can be reduced. The important principle remains, however, that all pupils are being posed the same questions, even if the amount of source material they are using is varied.

Strategies such as these should ensure that all pupils end up succeeding (at their own level) with each of the tasks in the book.

It is also important that pupils are not left alone to tackle each enquiry. The book has been written with the expectation that much of the material in the authors' text will be introduced by the teacher. It might be that the teacher reads a spread through beforehand and then uses the information it provides to set the scene for pupils, before they proceed to the sources and questions.

It is also sound practice to read and discuss all the sources with pupils. We are attempting to develop pupils' skills and understanding, which will not be achieved by simply leaving them to get on with the questions by themselves all the time.

Group work can also help here. Some pupils will contribute to a small group discussion, and risk putting forward ideas and answers, in a way which they would not do in front of the whole class. We have all seen how pupils tend to experiment more in small groups, partly because they are not so worried about getting things wrong.

In this book pupils are working with new ideas, skills and problems for much of the time and we should not be surprised if their early attempts to answer a question fall well below what might be regarded as a good answer. However, any genuine attempts to tackle the questions should be encouraged – the teacher can then begin to suggest how such answers could be built on. If pupils are worried about 'getting it wrong' they will play safe and their progress will be hindered.

The third term

Our research has shown what a very wide range of choices schools are considering for the third term of Y8. Some schools will be studying a Category C unit, some will be studying a Category A unit. Others may be starting their Y9 course early to ensure coverage of the two core units before SATs in Y9, or to allow **Britain and the Great War** to be studied in its chronological place in Y9.

We have therefore left a wide range of options open for this third term. However, our suggestion is that you use it to develop the theme of 'societies in change' still further. There are a range of possibilities to consider.

Category A
- **A local history unit:**
One of the most promising longer-term possibilities, once schools have had the opportunity and the time to gather local resources relating to the British core units, is to design your own local history unit using local resources to investigate change in your area.

A sense of local chronology – of change over time in the local area – can help motivate pupils towards a broader interest in History and make them feel more fully a part of their local community.

Over the coming years, pupils will also be coming into Key Stage 3 with a substantial amount of local history awareness from the work they have done in Key Stage 2 History and Geography. This can be built on and developed in Key Stage 3.

The detailed notes for The Making of the UK include many suggestions for local study which can be used to develop a local history unit. Possibilities exist in all of the following enquiries: *Were the poor really poor?*, *Were the rich really rich?*, *Henry VIII: Catholic or Protestant* (local work on a pre-Reformation monastery), *The Reformation in English villages*, *Who fought whom?* (the Civil War loyalties of the various social groups in your local area, including leading gentry), *What was life like during the Civil War?* (local battles, stories and case studies), *How did London change?* (which in itself can be used as the basis for a study of change in the local area by schools in London), *A Tour through Britain*.

The emphasis in the local study should be on how the area changed between 1500 and 1750 and could embrace one of the themes covered in this unit, e.g. the poor and the rich, the Reformation, or the Civil War. The focus should be on detailed work, something pupils can get into in depth.

Many different local resources can be used: documents, such as court rolls, Tudor enclosure records or wills; buildings, such as almshouses and the inscriptions on them, manor houses and mansions; portraits and paintings; maps; artefacts from your county museum, etc.

Pupils could split into groups to study different aspects of change in the local area.

An alternative local history unit would be as suggested in the Category A list in the final orders for NC History – 'The impact of the Industrial Revolution on a local area'. In schools in Britain's industrial heartland this would be a natural unit both to develop further the ideas dealt with in *Societies in Change* and to set pupils up with an understanding of industrial change in a specific place to form a background for their study of **Expansion, Trade and Industry** in Y9.

■ Britain and the Great War:

This supplementary unit studies the way the Great War changed British society, in particular the position of women.

Using it at the end of Y8 would prevent the war being studied in its chronological context (between **Expansion, Trade and Industry** and **The Era of the Second World War**), but it would have the advantage of allowing pupils to study an example of war as a trigger of social change, to compare with the other political and religious factors which *Societies in Change* focused on.

■ The Changing Role of Women:

This supplementary unit focuses on British History – reviewing the periods studied in the British core units – and examines how and why the respective roles of women and men changed during these periods.

It is a long-term development study, which has its beginnings in Roman Britain yet which takes pupils into the changes that occurred during the nineteenth century and into the twentieth century, including the significance of the Great War. It therefore sets pupils up with a useful perspective on the developments which will be studied in the core units in Y9.

Category C
■ India under the Mughals:

A study of change in a non-European culture. It investigates the relative importance of external influences and internal pressures in bringing about change. It also investigates the meeting of two cultures.

Chronologically it fits well between the Y8 units and the core unit **Expansion, Trade and Industry** and it also illuminates one aspect of that core unit – the growth of

the British Empire – from the perspective of the countries that were colonised by Britain.

■ Black Peoples of the Americas:

This unit investigates the changes that occurred for black people over several centuries, particularly in the Caribbean and the United States.

It links in well with the work on **The Making of the UK** and, like Mughal India, it provides a strong base for the study of **Expansion, Trade and Industry**.

From these five possibilities it will be clear that the theme of 'societies in change' is capable of being developed in many different ways. This ensures that you have great flexibility to vary your *Societies in Change* course within a school or from year to year and to tailor it to the background, needs and interests of your pupils.

CROSS-CURRICULAR LINKS

This book will make a very useful contribution to cross-curricular learning. We have mentioned just a few examples below to illustrate the possibilities. Others are discussed further in the detailed notes.

Themes

In The Making of the UK we are investigating periods of British History in which the UK and many of its modern political structures began to take shape. This gives plentiful opportunities, therefore, for developing education for citizenship.

The executions of Kings Charles I and Louis XVI point to important questions about the relationship of the monarchy to Parliament and the people.

Both units give opportunities for comparing past political systems with our system today. Which is more democratic and why? The attempted democratic reforms of the French Revolution are compared with our system in Britain today – contrasting, for example, who is elected and by whom.

Other broader citizenship questions are raised in the French Revolution unit: the rights and wrongs of using violence to bring about change, the consequences of inequality within society and the problems that the citizens and citizenesses (they did use that term in the eighteenth century) faced as they attempted to put their ideals into practice.

Family life in the sixteenth and seventeenth centuries is looked at in detail in The Making of the UK. We raise many issues which can lead to fruitful comparisons with today: gender roles within the family, family relationships, housing. These enquiries also offer an interesting perspective on health education and on childcare today. In the work on the treatment of the poor in the sixteenth century we also raise issues to do with the support and care of the poor which have strong resonances today, when the role of the government in welfare provision is continually under scrutiny.

Finally, both units gave opportunities for furthering pupils' economic and industrial understanding – for example, in advising the King of France on his budgeting problems, or in assessing the varying impact of different forms of taxation.

Religious Studies

Both units also investigate important themes in Religious Studies.

In The Making of the UK, disputes about religious beliefs and practices are central to the sections on the Reformation and the Civil War. Pupils can begin to appreciate the power of religious issues in societies of the past and to make comparisons with the significance of religious issues in society today.

In both units, there are examples of the problems raised when one religion or one denomination has favoured status over others. This raises the contemporary question of why Christianity has favoured status in Britain today, and whether that is a good thing or not.

There are plentiful opportunities for investigating issues of personal and social education. For example, the case studies of the seventeenth-century witch hunts can be developed as a broader study of the prejudice and fear that gave rise to them. Religious persecution – of Protestants in Mary's reign, of Catholics in Elizabeth's and James' reigns, of the Puritans before the Civil War – also raises important and relevant questions for religious education.

Other NC subjects

Finally, there are many links into other core and foundation subjects. For example:

■ Science: the seventeenth-century Scientific Revolution is introduced; the ways in which scientific change led to change in other areas of society are investigated in both units.

■ Geography: the book provides a valuable historical perspective on themes in Geography AT4, such as urbanisation and the growth and development of settlements (both in the case study of London, pages 82–87), and transport networks and location of industry (in Defoe's tour of Britain, pages 88–93).

The Making of the UK also lays a framework for understanding Britain's pattern of trade with the rest of the world, which will be further developed in Y9 studies and which can contribute to work in Geography AT2.

■ English: there are plenty of opportunities for working in collaboration with colleagues in the English department on an investigation of aspects of the Elizabethan theatre.

Some pupils may be keen to develop their understanding of the period by further reading. We have provided here a reading list of historical fiction which illuminates events or themes covered in the two units. These books may be available through English departments or libraries, and can be used as part of pupils' work with English literature as well as for their historical value. Such books also provide useful material for History ATs 2 and 3.

The Making of the UK

Cue for Treason by Geoffrey Trease (the Tudors)
The King's Beard by L. Wibberley (Elizabethan period) (Faber)
Beat the Drum by A.S. Wood (Elizabethan period) (Hodder & Stoughton)
The Armourer's House by Rosemary Sutcliff (Elizabethan period) (OUP)
Stars of Fortune by Cynthia Harnett (Elizabethan period/ Mary, Queen of Scots) (Methuen)
The Wonderful Winter by M. Chute (Elizabethan London) (Phoenix House)
Rich Inheritance, a trilogy by Winefride Nolan (the family fortunes of Catholic recusants) (Macmillan)
The Spaniards are coming by R. Manning-Sanders (the Spanish Armada) (Heinemann)
Fireships Away: the inside story of the Spanish Armada by H.T. Sutton (National Trust)
Simon by Rosemary Sutcliff (the English Civil War) (OUP)
Edge by M. Price (Battle of Edge Hill) (Rex Collings)
The Orange Sash by J. Dymoke (the English Civil War) (Jarrolds)
Fire over London by E. Leyland (the Great Fire) (Hutchinson)
The Great House by Cynthia Harnett (town and country life in the 1690s) (Methuen)
The Grey Pilot by A. MacVicar (Bonnie Prince Charlie) (Burke)
Lanterns over Lune by Kathleen Fidler (Bonnie Prince Charlie) (Lutterworth)

The French Revolution

A Tale of Two Cities by Charles Dickens
The Scarlet Pimpernel by Baroness Orczy
The Gods are Athirst by Anatole France

ASSESSMENT

How do we deal with the Attainment Targets?

The book is packed full of enquiries and questions. Most of them focus on one particular area of the ATs: in The Making of the UK, for instance, *Bloody Queen Mary?* (pages 32–33) is geared towards AT2. In The French Revolution, *Did the Revolution make France a fairer country?* (pages 118–121) is geared towards AT1 strand a. But in these enquiries, as in every enquiry, other ATs are covered as well. The course avoids artificially compartmentalising the ATs: the decision as to which of the ATs should be the focus of an enquiry has been determined by what the content requires, not by what the ATs stipulate.

Those of you who have used our Y7 material will now be familiar with our approach to the Attainment Targets. The Statements of Attainment are treated as a bank of skills and ideas which are used in History. They are important ideas, which we want pupils of all abilities to grapple with.

Although there is progression overall in the Attainment Targets (in each case level 10 is more demanding than level 1), this does not mean that each statement is progressive from the one before it. There are indeed places where pupils will need a reasonable grasp of one level to proceed to the next. For example, in AT1b, a pupil will need to grasp the ideas in level 3 to be able to grapple with level 4. But this is not always the case. Sometimes the natural progression leaps between levels, e.g. from AT1 strand b level 2 to AT1 strand c levels 6 and 7. At other times, one statement is subsumed by another statement: AT1c level 3, for example, will usually be implied by AT1a level 3.

The most important thing is to realise that each of the statements can be tackled at many different levels of achievement.

This has important implications for how we teach History:

■ It's not necessary (or desirable) to introduce the statements in the order they are laid down in the Final Orders.

■ Once pupils have achieved a given level in a particular AT, you do not then leave that level behind. You return to it regularly but make the work on it more demanding.

■ You can still introduce pupils to statements which the theory of the National Curriculum says are outside the scope of Y8, i.e. levels 7–10.

■ It is quite possible that pupils will touch on levels quite high up the scale, but in a relatively simple way, throughout their Key Stage 3 course.

So if each statement can be tackled at varying levels of difficulty, what is it that determines the level of difficulty of an exercise?

Points to consider are:
■ the amount of source material used
■ the complexity of the source material
■ the complexity of the events being studied
■ how familiar pupils already are with the content
■ how the content is structured
■ how the exercise is structured
■ whether pupils work individually or in groups
■ whether they respond orally, visually or in writing.

Clearly, *Societies in Change* cannot allow for all these variables in designing its questions and activities, but it can help you by structuring exercises, choosing source material and selecting content, and revisiting Statements of Attainment in such a way that the exercises do become progressively harder as you move through the course. We have worked hard to ensure that there is real progression both from Y7 to Y8 and within Y8.

In summary, what this book provides is a range of exercises which first introduce pupils to historical ideas and then keep spiralling back to those ideas to test how pupils deal with them in a range of contexts and with a range of content.

How do the enquiries access the levels of attainment?

The matrix on page 14 summarises how each enquiry in the book accesses the Statements of Attainment. It shows you at a glance where the emphasis of each unit and each enquiry lies.

More detailed question by question information is given in the 'AT boxes' which appear in the detailed notes for each enquiry. They show at a glance how each of the questions can access various levels of attainment. However, it is important to recognise that this can only be a rough guide. The statements are interlinked and, more importantly, are capable of very broad interpretation, so don't be surprised if pupils perform at levels, or even in ATs, that you did not anticipate.

Y7 experience has shown there is a tendency for teachers to fall back on questions which are targeted on just one level and which almost mirror the wording of that Statement of Attainment. This is to be avoided – especially if it's the only approach used. A diet of such questions is extremely dull for pupils: many of them look as if they've been taken straight off an examination paper!

Societies in Change, by contrast, offers a variety of techniques: some questions are closely targeted, while others are very open-ended.

One of the biggest challenges facing us in teacher-based assessment is to devise interesting, imaginative and open-ended tasks which do access the ATs and Statements of Attainment. The difficulty with such tasks is that it is not always apparent, at the time when the task is set, precisely which statements will be accessed. It is therefore as important as ever to study pupils' responses carefully, and in collaboration with other users of this material. We have indicated the intended aims of each task, but don't be surprised if there is evidence of statements which were not originally in the aims. If they are there in the pupils' work they should be rewarded.

With that proviso we can look at a few examples from the book to explain the thinking that has gone into the design of questions and tasks.

■ The majority of questions are designed to access a range of levels within an AT. You can see this immediately by looking through the AT boxes in the detailed notes. This is not to say that pupils will produce neatly packaged answers corresponding to each of the Statements of Attainment shown, or that they will demonstrate achievement at every level. What it does mean is that the question allows them access to all those levels. For example, in question 4 on page 9 of The Making of the UK, pupils consider how the government's treatment of the poor changed over the sixteenth century (AT1 strand a). To support their answer pupils need to consider what has changed (level 3), whether some things did not change (level 4) and whether the changes constitute progress or not (level 6).

- There are also many groups of questions which, taken together, access a wide range of levels within an AT: for example, questions 1–4 on page 16, in which pupils investigate the kinds of evidence available for us as we study the private lives of people who lived 400 years ago. Each separate question aims at a particular level. However, taken together, pupils' answers to these questions – in class discussion or small group work – will give you a feel for their understanding of a wide range of ideas within AT3. In such situations the total is more than the sum of the parts.
- Finally, most of the summary questions and activities access more than one AT. For example, the activity on page 69, while looking deceptively simple, allows access to a range of levels within all three strands of AT1. The best pupils will write letters which explain how post-Civil War society is changing (strand a), the reasons the changes have come about and why people are behaving as they are (strand b), and how the viewpoint of the gentry might be influenced by their circumstances (strand c).

On pages 14–19 we have provided two matrices. As already mentioned, the matrix on page 14 matches each enquiry to the Statements of Attainment. On pages 16–19 we have reproduced the list of statutory Statements of Attainment. Alongside each appropriate statement we have shown an example of how a question in the book accesses that statement.

These questions, like all others in the book, are designed to help develop pupils' understanding of the skills and ideas in each of the Statements of Attainment. As the introduction will have made clear, pupils must keep spiralling back to each statement throughout the course.

This table also serves to illustrate the wide range of techniques that can be used to access the various levels.

Teacher-based assessment and recording achievement

There will be two forms of assessment in Key Stage 3: SATs, which will not be used until the end of Y9, and teacher-based assessment, which will be used *throughout* the Key Stage.

- SATs:
At the time of writing Y9 SATs are being developed and trialled by an agency appointed by the government. The government has asked for 'pencil and paper' tests which all pupils would sit at the beginning of the summer term of Y9. There would be two one-hour tests.

The agency has been asked to investigate two possible models for these tests: Model 1, which would assess pupils' knowledge of three core units, and Model 2, which would assess pupils' knowledge of two core units *plus* their breadth of knowledge across all five Key Stage 3 core units.

The almost inevitable outcome, whichever model is finally adopted, is that in many schools Y9 will be devoted to the final two Key Stage 3 core units, **Expansion, Trade and Industry** and **The Era of the Second World War**. Therefore, the *Discovering the Past* Y9 core text,

Peace and War, will include these final two core units. It will also provide full preparation for the Y9 SATs, whatever they may demand.

- Teacher-based assessment:
In Y8, however, we are continuing to concentrate on teacher-based assessment.

One aim of this book – and of the series – has been to encourage the integration of teacher-based assessment into normal classroom teaching. We have taken the view that as far as is practicable teacher-based assessment should be continuous. It should not be a separate activity, using additional or different tasks. The tasks used for assessment purposes should be part of the teaching programme and an integral part of normal lessons.

Teacher-based assessment should certainly not be based on a test, which can only give a snapshot of pupil performance at one moment in time. It should take note of pupil performance in group work and oral work as well as in written work.

In addition, the ideal assessment system should provide flexibility as Key Stage 3 assessment takes shape over the coming years, make for a minimum of record keeping and provide a basis for teacher moderation of pupils' work.

- Recording how the ATs are accessed:
The questions and enquiries in this book are primarily designed to create learning opportunities for pupils in relation to the ATs. The matrix on page 14 summarises how the ATs are accessed, and a copy of it can also be used to record a class's coverage of the ATs for the benefit of interested parents or governors. Simply enter a date in the right-hand column to record when the enquiries are completed and thus which ATs have been accessed as the class progresses through the course.

- Recording achievement:
Pupils' oral and written work in response to the questions in the pupils' book will also provide the evidence you need to be able to make a *provisional* judgement about the attainment of each pupil at the end of Y8.

The statements are not hurdles to be cleared once and for all. Teacher-based assessment requires judgement over a period of time, based on a range of evidence. As part of the process of gathering this evidence about pupils' attainment the record sheet on pages 20–21 can be photocopied onto A3 paper and used to record pupils' work. It is obviously unrealistic to try to record everything the pupils do, so a balanced selection of a dozen or more tasks tackled during Y8 should be selected for recording purposes.

However, don't expect the record sheet itself to tell you which level each pupil has satisfactorily reached. It is only a tool to help you reach your own conclusion. Whether a pupil has reached level 4 or level 5 by the end of Key Stage 3 will always be a matter for you and your colleagues to decide, using your professional judgement based on your own knowledge of the pupil.

What the pupil record will give you is a raw profile of a pupil's achievement in each AT across the year. (You will need to create a departmental policy as to whether you record all statements a pupil has shown understanding of in completing a task, or only the highest level within each AT.) This evidence can then be interpreted in the light of your own knowledge of individual pupils.

For example, a pupil's recorded attainment in AT3 might look like this: levels 3, 5, 3, 4, 7, 3, 3, 2, 4, 1, 3, 4. On closer scrutiny, the record might reveal that on the occasions when level 1 and level 2 were recorded the questions were in fact specific to those levels. The pattern that therefore emerges from this profile is that the pupil can consistently operate at level 3.

However, there are some instances of level 4 being achieved. Using your own professional knowledge of the pupils based on all the work you have seen them do, including their contributions to class discussion, group work and oral work, as well as written work, you may well conclude that this pupil can cope well with level 4, and therefore you may award him/her that level.

Implicit in this latter process of professional judgement is that teachers will need to interpret the Statements of Attainment. This will involve meeting with colleagues from other schools to discuss what characterises satisfactory performance at a given level.

NC assessment is still in its developmental stages and we don't yet know what kind of answers are going to merit the award of a certain level, because the statements themselves are capable of broad interpretation. Take AT3 level 3 for example. The statement says 'Makes deductions from historical sources'. How do we decide what constitutes satisfactory performance at this level? Clearly some deductions are easier to make than others, and some sources are more complex to work with than others.

In comparing pupils' answers you will need to bear in mind at least two main variables – the *context* in which the pupil has completed the work and the *criteria* set for the work:

■ The context: Was there much guidance given in class beforehand? Were the sources discussed in class first? How complex was the source material? Was the question a closely directed one, e.g. 'What can you learn from this picture about how people at that time cooked their food?', or a more open-ended one, e.g. 'What can you learn about people at that time from this picture?'

■ The criteria: What was expected of the pupils? Were they asked to make a single deduction or more than one deduction? Were they expected to refer back to the source in explaining their deductions?

As pupils make progress in History, the support and guidance given should be reduced and the sources used should become more challenging. A greater breadth and depth of knowledge will be expected in pupils' work, and, finally, the criteria for the task can be made more demanding.

However, at this stage there are no satisfactory answers to the question of how the context should be set for level 3 work, or what criteria should be set for level 3 work. This will continue to emerge from the moderation process that is now well under way, based on comparison of actual pupil work in response to a wide variety of tasks and questions.

Once consensus has emerged as to what constitutes performance at a given level, pupils will have to perform at that level on a number of occasions across all the Y8 units before that level can be awarded.

■ Marking pupils' work:
Although keeping track of levels achieved is important for the teacher's record, there appears to be little point in talking to the pupils in terms of levels, or in marking their work level 2 or level 3. However, the skills and concepts in the Statements of Attainment should be mentioned. For example, if the question was 'What does this picture tell you about the people it shows?' there is little point in marking a pupil's work at AT3 level 1. What would be useful would be a comment such as 'A good detailed description of what the people in the picture are wearing. Can you try to use this to work out whether they were rich or poor?'. What this comment is actually doing is trying to encourage the pupil to move from level 1 to level 3 without confusing her about the numbers of the levels.

Teacher-based assessment will continue to evolve over the next few years. The Schools History Project is already involved with a number of LEAs in organising meetings for teachers to discuss and compare pupils' work and to make provisional judgements about pupils' attainment. If you want to find out more about what the project can offer for assessment INSET, contact the Schools History Project at the address on page 1 of this book.

	AT1 strand a – Change										AT1 strand b – Cause									
	1	2	3	4	5	6	7			10	1	2	3	4	5	6	7	8	9	10

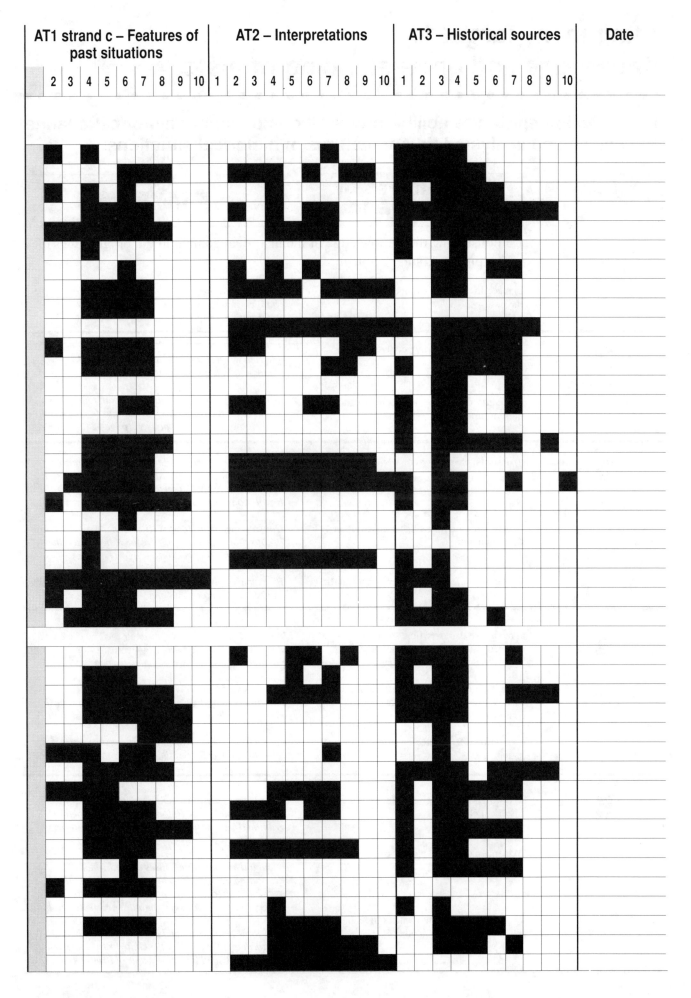

AT1 strand c – Features of past situations									AT2 – Interpretations										AT3 – Historical sources										Date
2	3	4	5	6	7	8	9	10	1	2	3	4	5	6	7	8	9	10	1	2	3	4	5	6	7	8	9	10	

Attainment Target 1:
Knowledge and understanding of history

●●

The development of the ability to describe and explain historical change and cause, and analyse different features of historical situations.

LEVEL	STATEMENTS OF ATTAINMENT	EXAMPLES
	Demonstrating their knowledge of the historical content in the programmes of study, pupils should be able to:	
1	a) place in sequence events in a story about the past.	*Make a timeline showing, in chronological order, the changes made to Melford Church during the Reformation. (page 35)*
2	b) suggest reasons why people in the past acted as they did.	*Consider why people in France might have been pleased when Napoleon and the army took over control of France in 1799. (page 147)*
	c) identify differences between past and present times.	*Compare the rooms and furnishings in pupils' own homes with the rooms and furnishings in seventeenth- and eighteenth-century houses. (page 12)*
3	a) describe changes over a period of time.	*In analysing a cartoon of the French Revolution, describe how the relationships between the peasants, nobles and clergy changed as a result of the Revolution. (page 120)*
	b) give a reason for an historical event or development.	*Consider whether Henry VIII closed the monasteries because they were corrupt, because he needed the money or for other reasons. (page 31)*
	c) identify differences between times in the past.	*By examining two drawings compare features of London in 1723 with features of London in 1500. (page 86)*
4	a) recognise that over time some things changed and others stayed the same.	*In pairs analyse aspects of French society to see which of the reforms of the Revolution were kept by Napoleon and which were changed. (page 150)*
	b) show an awareness that historical events usually have more than one cause and consequence.	*From a set of eight cartoons showing causes and consequences of the English Revolution, distinguish which is which and explain each one. (Worksheet 17)*
	c) describe different features of an historical period.	*In role as a counter-revolutionary, write a letter describing a member of the sans-culottes. (page 139)*
5	a) distinguish between different kinds of historical change.	*In a class discussion, decide which of the changes brought about by the Reformation were immediate, gradual, local, national, short-term or long-term (page 35).*
	b) identify different types of cause and consequence.	*From a list of possible causes of the French Revolution decide which are causes which built up over a long period and which causes actually triggered people to go out onto the streets. (page 117)*
	c) show how different features in an historical situation relate to each other.	*Find three similarities and three differences between the north and the south of the United Kingdom from the evidence provided by Defoe's tour of Britain. (page 93)*

LEVEL	STATEMENTS OF ATTAINMENT	EXAMPLES
6	a) show an understanding that change and progress are not the same.	*In considering whether the Revolution made France a fairer country, investigate whether the position of women and of slaves changed for the better. (page 121)*
	b) recognise that causes and consequences can vary in importance.	*From a set of events on a timeline, select five events which were important steps leading to union between England and Scotland. (page 72)*
	c) describe the different ideas and attitudes of people in an historical situation.	*Decide which of the reasons for discontent in pre-Revolutionary France would have most worried a peasant, a noblewoman, an urban worker and a businessman. (page 112)*
7	a) show an awareness that patterns of change can be complex.	*Taking into account case studies of scientific progress, medicine and health and the witch hunts, consider whether there was in fact a 'Scientific Revolution' in the seventeenth century. (page 81)*
	b) show how the different causes of an historical event are connected.	*Working in groups, compare the respective contributions of Russia, Spain and Britain to the defeat of Napoleon. (page 162)*
	c) show an awareness that different people's ideas and attitudes are often related to their circumstances.	*In a role-play based on the trial of Charles I, weigh up the differing views of witnesses speaking for and against Charles. (page 60)*
8	b) explain the relative importance of several linked causes.	*From a set of options choose those which best explain the reasons for the failure of the Jacobite Rebellion of 1745. (page 77)*
	c) show an understanding of the diversity of people's ideas, attitudes and circumstances in complex historical situations.	*Write a letter from a member of the gentry in 1650 describing the new radical ideas emerging in England after the Civil War and explaining which ideas the gentry are most worried about. (page 69)*
9	b) Show an understanding of how causes, motives and consequences may be related.	*Working in pairs create two posters from a Parliamentary and Royalist point of view explaining whose fault the Civil War was. (page 49)*
	c) explain why individuals did not necessarily share the ideas and attitudes of the groups and societies to which they belonged.	*In writing an obituary of Charlotte Corday, consider why she might have decided to assassinate the popular leader of the French Revolution Jean-Paul Marat. (page 143)*

Attainment Target 2:
Interpretations of history

●●●

The development of the ability to understand interpretations of history.

LEVEL	STATEMENTS OF ATTAINMENT	EXAMPLES
	Demonstrating their knowledge of the historical content in the programmes of study, pupils should be able to:	
2	show an awareness that different stories about the past can give different versions of what happened.	*Working in pairs, use evidence provided to create two newspaper front pages – one portraying Cromwell as someone out to grab power for himself, the other portraying Cromwell as acting in the best interests of England. (page 67)*
3	distinguish between a fact and a point of view.	*Identify how a nineteenth-century author writing a description of the Gunpowder Plot has shown her opinions of the Catholics. (page 36)*
4	show an understanding that deficiencies in evidence may lead to different interpretations of the past.	*Suggest reasons why a cartoon showing the situation of women before the French Revolution is not used as often as a similar cartoon showing the situation of men. (page 108)*
5	recognise that interpretations of the past, including popular accounts, may differ from what is known to have happened.	*Using a range of sources, compare the historical significance of the Bastille with its significance in popular accounts of the French Revolution. (page 99)*
6	demonstrate how historical interpretations depend on the selection of sources.	*Select from a range of sources about marriage between 1500 and 1750 those that support a given historian's point of view. (page 17)*
7	describe the strengths and weaknesses of different interpretations of an historical event or development.	*Consider two conflicting assessments of Robespierre and test them against other evidence. (pages 144–145)*
8	show how attitudes and circumstances can influence an individual's interpretations of historical events or developments.	*In looking at two posthumous portraits of Elizabeth I, consider why interpretations of her might have changed between 1605 and 1625. (pages 40–41)*
9	explain why different groups or societies interpret and use history in different ways.	*Compare the differing attitudes to the significance of the French Revolution of three twentieth-century political leaders (from Nazi Germany, the Communist Soviet Union and modern Britain). (pages 168–169)*
10	show an understanding of the issues involved in trying to make history as objective as possible.	*Consider how the interpretation of Queen Mary's reign given by Foxe's Book of Martyrs has influenced our view of Mary today and attempt to reach a more objective view. (pages 132–133)*

Attainment Target 3:
The use of historical sources

• •

The development of pupils' ability to acquire evidence from historical sources, and form judgements about their reliability and value.

LEVEL	STATEMENTS OF ATTAINMENT	EXAMPLES
	Demonstrating their knowledge of the historical content in the programmes of study, pupils should be able to:	
1	communicate information acquired from an historical source.	*In studying pictures of life in the 1500s, describe in detail what is going on in each picture. (pages 3–5)*
2	recognise that historical sources can stimulate and help answer questions about the past.	*Consider what kind of sources are available to us for studying people in the sixteenth and seventeenth centuries. (page 16)*
3	make deductions from historical sources.	*Decide what message a cartoon of the French Revolution is intended to convey. (page 108)*
4	put together information drawn from different historical sources.	*Draw a map to show what happened at the Battle of Marston Moor using a range of primary and secondary sources. (pages 56–57)*
5	comment on the usefulness of an historical source by reference to its content, as evidence for a particular enquiry.	*From various portraits of Elizabeth I, choose one which is most useful for showing us what she really looked like. (pages 40–41)*
6	compare the usefulness of different historical sources as evidence for a particular enquiry.	*Compare the value of different sources for helping to work out Louis' real reasons for fleeing from Paris. (page 124)*
7	make judgements about the reliability and value of historical sources by reference to the circumstances in which they were produced.	*Consider Napoleon's official account of the* Coup de Brumaire *and compare it with other accounts by his enemies and supporters. (pages 147–148)*
8	show how a source which is unreliable can nevertheless be useful.	*Consider what a picture that wrongly shows Napoleon's mother attending his coronation might suggest about Napoleon and his motives. (page 149)*
9	show an understanding that a source can be more or less valuable depending on the questions asked of it.	*Consider whether a group of sources can together give reliable evidence about some aspects of Charles I's execution but not about others. (page 60)*
10	explain the problematic nature of historical evidence, showing an awareness that judgements based on historical sources may well be provisional.	*In considering two contrasting newspaper reports on Oliver Cromwell, show an awareness of the difficulty of reaching a definitive judgement on his actions. (page 67)*

RECORD OF ACHIEVEMENT
HISTORY ATTAINMENT TARGETS 1, 2 AND 3

Date	Description of activity (including levels accessed)	AT1: KNOWLEDGE AND UNDERSTANDING OF HISTORY													
		a) Change							b) Cause						
		1	2	3	4	5	6	7	1	2	3	4	5	6	7
	THE MAKING OF THE UK														
	THE FRENCH REVOLUTION														

SCHOOL:

PUPIL'S NAME: .... CLASS: ....

c) Features of past situations							AT2: INTERPRETATIONS OF HISTORY								AT3: USE OF HISTORICAL SOURCES							COMMENTS
2	3	4	5	6	7	1	2	3	4	5	6	7	1	2	3	4	5	6	7	

THE MAKING OF THE UK

Introduction

The Making of the UK is a core unit in the National Curriculum. You can see from the matrix on page 5 how the required content is covered by the pupils' book.

The unit begins by helping pupils to capture the flavour of life in this period by looking at the poor and the rich, at aspects of family life and at entertainments (Section 2). This section should allow pupils to reconstruct an overall picture of life in the period before they go on to study the English Reformation (Section 3), the English Civil War (Section 4) and the union of the United Kingdom (Section 5).

Throughout the unit there are extensive opportunities for introducing local examples and local studies, and even the opportunity to design a separate local history study unit if you wish (described in more detail on page 8).

THE ATTAINMENT TARGETS

This unit gives access to each strand of the Attainment Targets.

Throughout the detailed notes the 'AT boxes' will show you which Statements of Attainment are intended to be accessed by the questions. However, as we have already stated in the general introduction, these suggested levels can only be a general guide. Experience shows that many of the questions and activities in the unit can lead some pupils to show attainment in other ATs and at other levels than we (or you) may have anticipated. When this happens credit should be given. It is important to look at pupil responses before finally deciding which ATs and levels are accessed.

■ The title of the course is *Societies in Change* and historical change (AT1 strand a) is a major theme of this unit, from the vacillations of religious change in a Suffolk village during the sixteenth century to an investigation of how the Civil War changed England.

Section 5 then picks up a number of case studies which span the whole period 1500–1750, and examine change over that period: political change (*How united was the United Kingdom?*), scientific and social change (*Science and superstition*), and demographic, economic and cultural change (*How did London change?*).

The unit concludes with a study of the United Kingdom as a whole, viewed through the eyes of Daniel Defoe, which allows pupils not only to appreciate the diversity of the UK in the eighteenth century, but also to consider the overall question of how the country had changed since 1500.

■ The Civil War is a watershed in English political history, with causes going back into the disputes between Parliament and monarch in earlier centuries and consequences stretching into present times. Work on causation (AT1 strand b) is therefore particularly focused on the Civil War enquiries in Section 4 such as *Why did civil war break out in 1642?* and *Why did the English execute their king?*.

■ The early part of the unit focuses on reconstructing life in the period (AT1 strand c). We investigate whether this period was a good time to be living in England and see how the answer to that question depended on many variables, such as who you were, where you were living and how rich you were.

■ There are opportunities to work towards AT2 throughout the unit, with some enquiries, such as those on Queen Mary, the Gunpowder Plot and the aftermath of Charles I's death, being particularly focused on AT2.

■ Evidence-based enquiry (AT3) is the mainstay of the unit, as it is of the entire *Discovering the Past* course in Key Stage 3.

Some enquiries have a distinct AT3 focus: *Private lives*, for example, takes the form of an extended debate with the modern historian Lawrence Stone. Pupils look at a wide range of primary sources to test some of his conclusions.

In The Making of the UK pupils will also begin to come into contact with some new and distinctive categories of source material – for instance, pamphlets and political cartoons with their heavy symbolism (e.g. pages 55 and 66 of the pupils' book).

The aim in this book, as it is throughout the series, is for pupils to have as much original source material to work with as possible, so that as they reach their conclusions about the past they will also be acquiring the skills to interrogate a wide range of source material. They will be working with visual sources such as engravings, paintings, drawings, plans, maps, photographs, artefacts, stained glass, reconstruction drawings and graphs, as well as a whole range of documentary source material: diaries, autobiographies, menus, laws, wills, writings, memoirs, government reports, letters, histories, confessions and newspaper articles.

FURTHER READING

General background reading for teachers:

Sixteenth-century England by Joyce Youings (Penguin) (part of the Pelican Social History of Britain, which is soon to include a volume on the seventeenth century)
The *Oxford History of England* covers the period circa 1500–1750 in five volumes

More specialised books for teachers:

Family, Sex and Marriage by Lawrence Stone (Penguin) (background to the *Private lives* enquiry)
The Blind Devotion of the People by Robert Whiting (CUP) (the Reformation among ordinary people, particularly in South-west England)
The Spoil of Melford Church: The Reformation in a Suffolk Parish by David Symond and Clive Paine (Salient Press)
Portraits of Queen Elizabeth by Roy Strong (OUP)
The English Civil War by Maurice Ashley (Alan Sutton)
The World Turned Upside Down by Christopher Hill (Penguin) (new ideas after the Civil War)
The Times London History Atlas (HarperCollins)

Detailed notes

Section 1: Introduction

ENQUIRY: ENGLAND IN THE 1500s

Pupils' Book pp. 2–5

With the benefit of hindsight 1500 might seem like some sort of watershed in British history. The Tudors were now established and England was moving into a period of consolidation and growth, with increasing worldwide influence.

However, that is hardly how the situation would have appeared to someone living at the time. Without hindsight it might seem that England in 1500 was little different from England in 1400 – even 1300. It was essentially rural and agricultural, and the threat of political instability was still current.

The starting point for this enquiry is to compare England in 1500 with what the pupils *do* know about – England today. The enquiry then moves on to establish a rounded picture of life in the 1500s which will allow pupils both to see continuity with medieval Britain and also to establish a base against which to judge some of the changes that will take place during the course of this unit.

The emphasis is on AT3 work. Pupils are working in depth with a wide range of visual sources. They should end up with some idea of the diversity of English society at that time, especially with regard to social classes and town life/country life.

(Pages 2–3)

Q1: AT1c level 2

Source 2: This is written in 1577 and yet describes changes in the lifetimes of old men living in an Essex village. Pupils can consider how this source helps us find out both about life in 1500 and about changes during the 1500s.

Source 4: Ask pupils if they think this is a typical meal. They will have done enough work on diet in the Middle Ages to judge.

Question 1: Best used for class discussion. Draw up comparative lists on the blackboard.

You could also discuss this general question: was England in 1500 more like England today or more like England in the Middle Ages?

Social groups

Q1: AT1c level 4, AT3 levels 1, 2, 3
Q2–3: AT3 level 3

The writer quoted is William Harrison.

Gentry: Draw pupils' attention to the glossary on page 170. Glossary words are printed in small capitals.

Questions 1–3: You could work through all three questions with the class as a whole, using just Source 5, to give pupils the feel for detailed interrogation of visual sources. Look closely at what is going on in the picture. What games are being played? What else is going on? Are the people rich or poor, or a mixture? Is this taking place in a town or in a village or in a city?

This detailed interrogation will set pupils up for more independent work with the visuals on the next spread.

(Pages 4–5)

Activity: AT2 level 7, AT3 levels 3, 4

Source 6: A farming scene. Notice how the artist has shown many different jobs going on at the same time: ploughing, sowing, harrowing, herding, forestry, etc. Notice also the plague of flies – or bees.

Source 7: An ingenious dockside crane – a crane of this model, driven by human power inside the treadmill, is described in use at Bristol docks.

Source 8: From a painting showing scenes in the life of Henry Unton – this is his wedding feast, showing musicians, dancers and dinner guests.

Source 9: A woman spinning. Notice the plainly furnished room, and also the houses outside the window – is this a town or a village?

Source 10: Death taking a baby, an engraving from the sixteenth century. Notice the simple fire for cooking, the damaged walls of the house, and the expressions of the woman and children.

Source 11: Mixing a balsam (an ointment) using plants, oils and herbs. One figure is selecting the ingredients, the other pounding them. The central figure is 'cooking' the balsam.

Source 12: From the Bradford Table Carpet, now in the Victoria and Albert Museum, which shows many scenes of sixteenth-century life. This section shows hunting and fishing.

Source 13: A barber's shop. Notice how the water for the shampoo is stored.

Source 14: A mine – a Swiss picture, but typical of mining techniques in sixteenth-century Britain. Notice the winding gear and the ladders into the mine.

Source 15: A sixteenth-century kitchen. Food is being spit roasted, firewood fetched, vegetables prepared, dishes washed, etc. A well dressed man in the centre is giving orders to the cooks.

Activity: This activity is designed to enable pupils to understand the diversity of English society and to prepare for Section 2 of the book, which asks 'Was this a good time to be living in England?'. It all depends on your social class, your wealth, where you lived, when you lived, your religion and many other variables besides.

It tests mainly AT3 skills, but class discussion could lead on to discussion of AT2 issues.

Section 2: Was this a good time to be living in England?

ENQUIRY: WERE THE POOR REALLY POOR?

Pupils' Book pp. 6–11
Worksheets 1, 2, 3

There were certainly many poor in Tudor England, and the writers and governments of the time were very worried about them. This three-spread enquiry investigates why governments were so worried about the poor, and what attempts were made over the period to deal with the problem of poor people.

The key question for the enquiry poses the dilemma facing the authorities of the time: were the poor *really* helpless, or were they just pretending to be helpless so that they could scrounge off richer people and live off charity?

This is an issue which has echoes throughout history and even today could raise a heated debate in the classroom, or for that matter in Parliament. Causes of poverty are seldom clear-cut or agreed upon by people of differing political persuasions.

(Pages 6–7)

Q1–3, 5: AT3 levels 1, 2, 3
Activity: AT1b level 2, AT1c level 6
Q4: AT1b level 2

Questions 1 and 2 are best used in a class discussion, rather than for written work. The same goes for the majority of questions in this enquiry, and in most of the enquiries, in fact.

Question 1: The illustrations have been chosen so that there are not always clear-cut answers. Picture 1 doesn't match closely to any of the descriptions, although pupils could reasonably argue for the beggar being a Rogue, or that he is genuinely poor and helpless – see the club foot.

Picture 2 = C, a Counterfeit Crank – the original caption read 'A soap-eater'

Picture 3 = E, a Clapper dudgeon (see bloody bandages on legs and arms)

Picture 4 = G, a Bawdy Basket

Picture 5 = B, an Upright Man

Picture 6 = A, a Rogue

Picture 7 = D, a Doxy

Picture 8 = F, an Abraham Man

Question 2: Pictures 1, 2 and 8 were drawn in the sixteenth century. Encourage pupils to explain how they distinguished between artist's reconstructions and primary sources.

The descriptions, likewise, are a mix of contemporary and modern: A, E and G are by sixteenth-century writers.

Activity: Worksheet 2 gives more information about Nicholas Jennings, who dressed as various kinds of beggar at various times. It covers AT3, but also gives opportunities to access AT1c. Pupils should be encouraged to emphasise what the authorities at the time would have been worried about.

Question 5: This is an opportunity to emphasise to pupils how selective sixteenth-century writers were. They spent much more time describing the poor who were pretending than describing the many who were really poor. Pupils can consider why there might be this 'bias'.

The houses of the poor

Q1: AT3 levels 3, 4

Source 4: Another inventory for another household is on page 14.

Question 1: This is the pupils' first sight of an inventory, so it is a good idea to go through Source 4 with them and discuss what it tells us about Thomas Herries. Pupils can then be left to make a comparison with Source 3 themselves.

(Pages 8–9)

Why were people poor?

Q1: AT3 levels 1, 3, 4
Q2: AT2 level 2
Q3: AT2 levels 3, 4, 6, 8, 9
Q4: AT3 level 3
Q5: AT1b levels 3, 4, 5, 6, 7, AT3 level 5
Activity: AT1b levels 2, 3, 4, 5, AT1c level 6, AT3 levels 1, 2, 3, 4

The elements of this enquiry range over the entire period 1500–1750. There is an overall timeline of the unit on page 1 of the pupils' book which you can refer to. It gives pupils a time map of the period. **Worksheet 1** can be copied for pupils to refer to.

Questions 4 and 5: Source 6 shows how bad or good the harvests were, as extrapolated by historians from prices of wheat in a given year. So in 1556, for instance, the price of wheat was double the average for the century, while in 1547 it was almost half the average for the century. However, for question 4 the detail of the graph is less important than the general impression it gives of troughs and peaks.

You can make clear to pupils how more expensive wheat would lead to more expensive bread. Bread was the staple part of most people's diet. Pupils must realise how dependent people were on bread and how desperate a situation could become if ordinary people could not afford bread. In Unit B of this book we will be examining how a bad harvest followed by an increase in the price of bread helped to trigger the French Revolution, as urban workers saw more than three quarters of their income going purely to buy bread – that is if they could get it at all (see page 114).

Question 5: Class discussion could bring out the types of causes and which were most important.

Activity: This is a major piece of work. Pupils will need to use a range of sources together (AT3), investigate causation at a range of levels (AT1b), and also attempt to see things from the JP's point of view (AT1c).

Worksheet 3 is the report by Edward Hext.

Justice of the Peace: Make sure pupils appreciate that JPs were the key figures in local government, with wide responsibilities. They were appointed by the king. They met in each county four times a year (thus 'Quarter Sessions'). Their decisions have been carefully recorded on 'rolls'. Many of these rolls still survive today and give us a very clear picture of the work of a JP. Typically they

■ collected money to keep bridges and roads in a good state
■ collected money to help people who had been crippled in war
■ granted licences to local tradesmen
■ collected hearth taxes (a tax based on the number of fireplaces in a house)
■ granted licences to alehouses
■ sorted out disputes between people
■ organised the investigation and arrest of criminals
■ tried all but the most serious offences. The most serious were handled by the assize judge.

There would be other officials helping the JP with local administration. These included the churchwarden, the constable (helped the JP with keeping law and order, collecting taxes and controlling beggars), the overseer of the poor, and the surveyor of the highway.

Once pupils' reports are written, discuss how the government might react to the letters – which is the subject of the facing page.

What did the government do about the poor?

Q2–3: AT1a levels 1, 3
Q4: AT1a levels 3, 4, 6
Q5: AT3 levels 3, 4
Q6: AT1b levels 2, 3, 4, AT1c levels 6, 7, 8

Question 1 raises citizenship and economic awareness issues. Most pupils will have views on, if not experience of, contemporary homelessness and poverty, which can be raised in a class discussion around question 1. This discussion will also form a good basis for discussing question 5.

Source 8: These Poor Laws are only a small selection of the many passed over the century.

Question 5: Assuming the date of Source 9 to be about 1550 or 1560 the man being whipped at the cart tail (B) could be a vagrant 'being whole in body . . . who can give no explanation how he lawfully gets his living' (see 1531 Act).

The man being hanged (A) could be a persistent vagrant who had been made a slave and who had twice run away from his master (see 1547 Act).

Question 6 might best be tackled through class discussion. The treatment of the poor is a useful context in which to explain that people in the past had different values and beliefs from ours today, and that this led them to do things which would be unacceptable today.

(Pages 10–11)

What did the towns do about the poor?

Q1–2: AT3 levels 3, 4

Question 1: Norwich, London and Ipswich have been chosen as among the biggest towns or cities of the time. If you can find evidence relating to your local area – e.g. documenting when the first almshouses were built or listing charitable donations, or local laws relating to the poor, etc. – introduce them here.

Question 2: The division between the government's and the town's responsibilities is not a clear-cut one. The government carried out most of its legislation through town and village officials. However, for the towns, poverty was a particular problem because the poor flocked to the towns in times of hardship looking for work or help (as they do throughout the world today). It was thus the towns which had the most immediate problem. They were the ones who in practice had to deal with the poor. They originated many of the measures for dealing with the poor which subsequently became government policy.

Q3–4: AT3 level 3

Questions 3 and 4: Breughel called this painting *The Parable of the Blind*, and like his other paintings it has a hard satirical edge to it. There are no right answers to these questions. There is scope for different deductions to be made. The most important element of pupils' answers will be the reasons given.

Did things improve in the seventeenth and eighteenth centuries?

Q1: AT3 levels 1, 2, 3
Q2–3: AT1a levels 1, 3, 4, 6, 7
Q4: AT1a levels 3, 4, 5, 6, 7

Question 2: Here also your own local examples would be very valuable.

Question 4: Make sure pupils explain their choice and discuss differences fully.

ENQUIRY: WERE THE RICH REALLY RICH?

Pupils' Book pp. 12–15

A two-spread enquiry which investigates a) how the houses and possessions of the rich at that time compare with the houses and possessions of ordinary people today, b) how the houses of the rich compared with the houses of the poor, and c) how life was changing for the rich during the sixteenth and seventeenth centuries. It thus covers a wide range of ideas in AT1c.

Questions 1–3 are designed as an easy introduction to the rest of the work.

(Pages 12–13)
The houses of the rich

Q1: AT3 levels 1, 3
Q2–3, 6: AT1c level 2
Q4–5: AT3 level 3

Questions 1 and 4: Source 1 is the long gallery from Hardwick Hall, Source 2 is the dining room from The Old House, Source 3 is the kitchen from Hardwick, Source 4 is the bedroom from The Old House.

Encourage pupils to explain their answers by referring to evidence in the photos rather than simply guessing – e.g. the leaded windows, the half timbering, the size of windows, the scale.

Questions 5 and 6: For class discussion. If you are able to get hold of some actual household items from a local museum or from your county archive office, all the better. Pupils will enjoy handling these objects.

Source 7 shows:
(top row, left to right)
- posy mats – sweet desserts would be served on them, and afterwards the mat would be turned over to reveal a rhyme or epigram (and make the table sticky)
- a child's feeding cup
- a wig stand
(bottom row, left to right)
- a hand stove or herb burner, used to sweeten the air
- pewter flagons and a plate
- shaving equipment.

(Pages 14–15)
Changes

Q1: AT1a level 3
Activity: AT3 level 3

Question 1: If pupils can refer back to their earlier work on the Middle Ages they will produce fuller answers to this question, but that is not the initial aim. The clues are in the narrative above, e.g. wooden panelling, fireplaces, kitchens, privacy, wood floors, patterned walls, four poster beds, etc.

Activity: Most AT3 level 3 work asks pupils to make deductions from visual sources and to express their findings in written work. This does it the other way round – deducing from a written description what the spit would have looked like.

A tradeswoman's house

Q1–2: AT3 levels 1, 3
Q3: AT2 level 4, AT3 levels 3, 4
Q4: AT3 level 3

Source 8: Inventories had values placed on each item – information needed for probate purposes. Pupils might consider what they think the most valuable items on this list might be. According to the lawyers' valuation it was the 82 tanned hides, valued at £48 out of a total probate value of about £100.

A merchant's house

Q1: AT1c level 2
Q2: AT1c level 4, AT3 level 4
Activity: AT1c levels 4, 6, AT3 level 4
Summary Activity: AT3 levels 5, 6

Sources 10 and 11: Pupils could be asked to compile an inventory for these rooms, to compare with the inventories on pages 7 and 14.

Activity: Bring in some Estate Agent's leaflets. It is important to stress to pupils that they should concentrate on what people at that time would be looking for.

Summary Activity: The important element is *why* the pupils choose certain things. For support work for some classes you might give them a selection of objects to choose from and ask them to explain and defend their choice.

Keep the results of this activity to compare with a similar activity in Unit B (see page 73 of these teachers' notes).

ENQUIRY: PRIVATE LIVES

Pupils' Book pp. 16–21

This three-spread enquiry is in the form of an extended debate with Lawrence Stone, whose *Family, Sex and Marriage in England, 1500–1800* is published in paperback by Penguin (Peregrine Books, 1982). Lawrence Stone was Professor of History at Oxford University until 1990.

The enquiry builds on the previous enquiries about the lives of the rich and the poor, although most of the evidence we have available to us deals with the rich.

(Pages 16–17)

Q1, 3: AT3 levels 2, 5
Q2: AT3 levels 5, 7, 8
Q4: AT3 levels 5, 6, 7, 8, 9

Questions 1–4: These questions are best used for class discussion. They make the important point that we simply do not have much evidence about private lives. You could ask the pupils whether a historian in 100 years' time will have more evidence about our private lives.

Getting married

Q1–2: AT3 levels 1, 3
Q3: AT2 level 4, AT3 level 4
Q4: AT2 levels 6, 7, AT3 levels 4, 5, 6
Q5: AT3 levels 1, 3
Q6: AT1b level 2, AT1c levels 6, 7

Questions 1 and 2: In some classes you may wish to limit this exercise to two sources only.
   Question 5: Include in the interrogation a discussion about whether pupils think this an upper-class wedding or a lower-class wedding.
   Question 6: This is a slightly compacted question which might need some elaboration. The reasons need to be generalised to a certain extent to make a modern comparison. Examples of reasons to get married are for love, because of parental pressure and being bought by someone; reasons not to include not enough money, not knowing each other well enough, not being in love and being too young. Arranged marriages, of course, remain the norm in some ethnic groups in the UK.

(Pages 18–19)

Being married

Q1, 2, 4, 7: AT3 level 3
Q3: AT1b level 2, AT1c level 6
Q5: AT1c level 6, AT2 level 2, AT3 level 7
Q6: AT1c level 6, AT3 level 4
Q8: AT3 levels 7, 8

Question 2: Flibbergib is the same word as the modern 'flibbertigibbet' – a flighty, restless person. A tattler is a gossip.
   Source 13: The date is 1678.

Privacy

If you have an opportunity to visit local houses or to bring in plans of local houses, you can put Lawrence Stone's ideas to the test. You could also ask you pupils to redesign a sixteenth-century house (like the one here) to give the occupants more privacy.

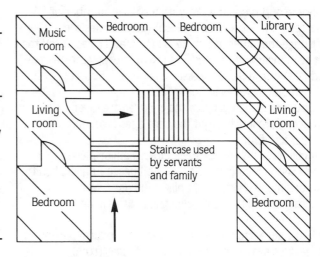

Key
   Doors
   Rooms used mainly by wife
   Rooms used mainly by husband
   Rooms used by other members of family

Having children

Q1: AT3 levels 1, 3

Question 1: Notice the unhygienic conditions, e.g. the dog, the chamber pot; notice the lack of privacy – the men eating their meal in the same room; notice the cradle on the floor – is this good for a baby or not? But notice also that the mother and child seem very well attended.

(Pages 20–21)

Q1: AT1c level 4
Q2: AT1a levels 3, 4, 6, 7, AT3 levels 3, 4, 5, 6
Activity: AT1a levels 3, 4, AT1c levels 4, 5, 6, AT3 level 4

The text is still based on Lawrence Stone's research and hypotheses. The aim on this spread is to check the hypotheses against the evidence we've provided.
   Question 2: Sources 16–25 may seem to present a bit of puzzle to start with. Begin with a class discussion around the two paragraphs above the question box. Break that down into a number of key points, e.g. better delivery methods, more love for children and breast-feeding replacing wet nursing, and ask pupils if they can find any evidence in Sources 16–25 either to confirm or deny the claims in that paragraph. The sources generally confirm improvements, but as with any representative set of sources from the time show that changes and improvement were not uniform or linear. How things improved depended on who you were: things changed at different rates for different people.

◆ ◆

Some pupils could work with a smaller number of sources (e.g. Sources 16 and 20) for this question.

Notice the skulls in Source 20 (the father has asked the artist to include them and to show him gazing at them in sadness), the children dressed as adults in Source 22 and the swaddled babies in Source 23.

Source 22: The ages of the children are given on the picture: from left to right they are aged two, one, six, five (twins) and four.

Activity: This could develop into a major piece of work, with cross-curricular possibilities in English, health education and childcare. Pupils could use a word processor and DTP to present the articles in an interesting way.

Make sure you have a few copies of modern 'parenting' magazines available for pupils to get ideas from.

ENQUIRY: COULD YOU ENJOY YOURSELF IN THE SIXTEENTH AND SEVENTEENTH CENTURIES?

Pupils' Book pp. 22–25
Worksheet 4

A two-spread enquiry that both challenges the view that there was no time for leisure in the sixteenth and seventeenth centuries, and also continues the twin themes that have been running through the section so far – comparing the lives of rich and poor, and comparing the habits of the period with the habits of today.

(Pages 22–23)

Q1–2: AT3 levels 1, 3
Q3: AT2 levels 4, 5, 6, 7, AT3 level 4
Q4–5: AT1c level 2
Q6: AT1c levels 4, 5, 6, AT2 level 6, AT3 level 4
Activity: AT1b level 2, AT1c levels 4, 5, 6, 7, AT3 level 4

Questions 1–3: Ideal for class discussion.

Source 1: Some definitions: 'decoy' – anything used to lure an animal into a trap, also a net covered pond; 'tumblers' and 'lurchers' are greyhounds trained to hunt; 'bat fowling' – hunting for bats; 'shovel board' – pushing coins on a board; 'goffe' – golf; 'shuttlecock' – badminton.

Source 2: The Puritans are mentioned in the source line. Their role is explored fully on pages 24–25.

Source 3: The first public theatre opened in London in 1576. At a time when theatre has become rather elitist, it may need emphasising that the theatre was a *popular* entertainment. Shakespeare's plays might have been seen by thousands of people every week, of all social classes. Point out the groundlings (ordinary people) and the rich people in the balconies.

Questions 4 and 5: You could select three entertainments for pupils to work with, e.g. Sources 3, 4 and 5.

(Pages 24–25)

The Puritans

Q1–2: AT3 levels 1, 3
Q3: AT3 level 7
Q4: AT1c level 6
Q5: AT1c levels 4, 5
Q6: AT3 levels 5, 6

Sources 9 and 10: Philip Stubbes was a Puritan pamphleteer. His *Anatomie of Abuses* (1583) is one of the most famous Puritan denunciations of customs and activities of the time (including football, May festivals and stage plays) which he considered needed abolishing.

Question 2 could lead to a discussion about the issue of Sunday trading – how far is this still a hangover from Puritan times? In Catholic countries which had no Puritan tradition Sunday trading is not an issue.

Questions 3–6: The criticisms in Sources 9–12 (Source 9 in particular) are quite subtle and difficult. They may need bringing out in class discussion:
- the worship of idols
- the violence of the sports
- godlessness and destroying Sunday
- a cover for plotters.

You could focus on just Sources 10 and 11 and still deal with the ideas in the questions.

Activity: AT1b level 8, AT1c levels 2, 3, 4, 5, 6, 7, 8, AT3 levels 3, 4

Activity: Some pupils might need a certain amount of guidance. **Worksheet 4** is a support worksheet to provide a structure for their research and suggest which sources they should consult.

Compare the statements drawn up by the pupils. In particular, draw out the contrasts between the lives of rich and poor people and the lives of men and women. Then discuss how to use the different statements to create a representative display of life in this period.

Pupils might like to use other categories for their statements.

Section 3: When was the English Reformation?

The sixteenth century was a time of immense religious upheaval. The next four enquiries take a broadly chronological journey through the sixteenth century, looking at religious changes brought in by successive Tudor monarchs from Henry VIII to Elizabeth. They build on one another and need to be seen together. They demonstrate vividly the complexities of change: in particular, how national changes are turned into local changes, and how after centuries of almost imperceptible movement change can happen at a dizzying speed.

They are followed by two more self-contained enquiries, on the Gunpowder Plot and Elizabeth – highly accessible work which will build on the understanding pupils will already have gained in Key Stage 2.

ENQUIRY: WAS THE CATHOLIC CHURCH STILL HEALTHY IN 1500?

Pupils' Book pp. 26–27
Worksheet 5

Many past historians have assumed that because there was a Reformation in the sixteenth century most people in England must have been dissatisfied with the Church. This spread gives pupils scope to question this interpretation. It sets up a picture of the pre-Reformation Church in England, still little changed from the Church in medieval times. Along with the subsequent enquiry on Henry VIII, it raises the question of whether the impetus for change came from below or above.

Q1: AT3 levels 1, 4
Q2: AT1b level 2
Activity: AT1c level 4, AT3 level 4

We are using Melford Church as a focus as we look at the changes brought about by the Reformation. The story of Melford has been written up in *The Spoil of Melford Church: the Reformation in a Suffolk Parish* by David Dymond and Clive Paine (Salient Press, 1989).

Source 1 will be compared with the post-Reformation church on page 31. Study and discuss it in detail in class to help set pupils up to understand Source 5. In particular, note the amount of decoration, the images and crucifixes, the vestments of the priest, the rood screen and rood screen loft, the altar furnishings, the Easter sepulchre (the alcove on the left).

Source 2: The window shows the seven sacraments, of which we have shown four. They are listed in the caption. You could ask pupils to spot which is which (*top left* Mass, *bottom left* marriage, *top right* baptism, *bottom right* last rites).

Question 1: Worksheet 5 reproduces Sources 5 and 6 for pupils to work with as homework. To make the task more accessible, you can complete a certain amount of the labelling yourself if you wish before making the photocopies.

ENQUIRY: HENRY VIII: CATHOLIC OR PROTESTANT?

Pupils' Book pp. 28–31

Although Henry VIII began great changes to the Catholic Church in England, he himself remained loyal to Catholic doctrines all his life. In this two-spread enquiry we investigate reasons for the break with Rome – were they religious or political? – and compare the changes made to the Church under Henry with the changes made under Edward VI.

Worksheet 1, the timeline of the period 1500–1750, can be used to illustrate the to-ing and fro-ing of the sixteenth-century Reformation.

(Pages 28–29)

Henry VIII

Q1–2: AT3 level 3
Q3: AT1b level 2, AT3 levels 3, 4
Activity: AT1c level 6, AT2 level 2, AT3 level 3

An everyday legacy of Henry's early commitment to the Catholic Church is on our coins: *FD* stands for Defender of the Faith, a title awarded to Henry by the Pope in 1521 in return for his vigorous defence of Catholicism against the Protestant teaching.

Questions 1 and 2 are for class discussion. You could use just Sources 1 and 2 for the comparisons.

Why did Henry close the monasteries?
Source 4: It will help pupils in their answers to questions 1–4 over the page if they have understood the way a monk was supposed to live.

Ask pairs of pupils to take one statement each from Source 4 and write a short entry for a monks' guidebook saying why monks are supposed to behave like this.

(Pages 30–31)

Q1–2: AT3 level 3
Q3–4: AT3 levels 3, 4, 6, 7
Q5: AT2 levels 4, 6
Q6: AT1b levels 2, 3, 4, 5, 6, 7

Source 5: You may be able to add evidence relating to a local monastery. Many of the reports have been published by historical record societies.

Edward VI

Activity: AT1a levels 3, 4, 5

Activity: Begin by comparing Source 11 with Source 1, which shows some very clear changes. Then extend the activity into a more general view of the Church as a whole by bringing in Sources 9 and 10.

ENQUIRY: BLOODY QUEEN MARY?

Pupils' Book pp. 32–33

A single-spread enquiry continuing the story of the English Reformation, or in this case Mary's attempts to bring back Roman Catholicism. It takes in AT2 work as pupils examine how our view of Mary has been influenced by the Protestant writer John Foxe.

Q1–4: AT1b levels 3, 4, 5, 6, 7

To help make the first point more strongly, draw a timeline from 1066 to 1553 which shows how long England had been Catholic and how long Protestant.

Questions 1 and 2 should be a group activity. Write each statement on a card, give each group a set, and ask pupils to sort them into two piles.

Mary's methods

Q1–4: AT3 levels 3, 4

Question 2: Source 2 *is* from the same book as Source 3.

Bloody Mary?

Q1: AT1c levels 4, 5, 6, 7
Q2: AT2 levels 2, 3, 4, 5, 7, 8, 9, 10

It is crucial for pupils to appreciate how during her reign people presumed Mary was succeeding.

Source 4: The full list of how many heretics were burned where is as follows: Morden 1, Rochford 1, Rayleigh 2, Brentwood 1, Maldon 1, Chelmsford 1, Colchester 23, Ipswich 5, Norwich 3, Beccles 3, Hadleigh 1, Thetford 3, Walsingham 1, Ely 1, Bury St Edmunds 12, Cambridge 1, Saffron Walden 1, Braintree 1, Barnet 3, London 74, Canterbury 40, Maidstone 7, Tunbridge 1, Ashford 2, Lewes 12, Winchester 1, Salisbury 3, Exeter 1, Bristol 5, Newbury 3, Oxford 3, Ware 1, Northampton 1, Leicester 1, Coventry 3, Gloucester 3, Hewent 1, Cardiff 1, Caermarthen 1, Haverford West 1, Lichfield 3, Derby 1, Chester 2, St Andrews 1, Edinburgh 20, Glasgow 2, Perth 6. Heretics were also burned in Chichester and St Albans.

Question 2 should be discussed in class before any written work is undertaken. It opens up the higher levels of AT2.

ENQUIRY: THE REFORMATION IN ENGLISH VILLAGES

Pupils' Book pp. 34–35

Changes at national level might take time to affect the village churches. In some parishes the changes were opposed or ignored for as long as possible. In this enquiry we focus again on Melford, to see how the changes affected the parish church there. We have also compared Melford with other parishes, and it would be ideal if you could introduce local examples for further comparison.

The Reformation in Melford Church

The cartoon represents most of the changes described in Sources 2–5. Ask pupils to describe what is going on in the cartoon before they look at the other sources.

Around the country

Q1: AT1a levels 1, 3, 4
Q2: AT1a level 5
Activity: AT1a levels 3, 4, 5, 7, AT1c levels 4, 5, 6, 7

Question 1: Write the following checklist on the board if necessary to help pupils recognise which features are Catholic and which not:

Features of Catholic churches
- Images
- Altars
- Candles
- Crucifixes
- Colourful wall paintings
- Rood screen
- Rood loft
- Sepulchre
- Surplices
- Vestments

Question 2: This targets a specific Statement of Attainment: AT1 strand a level 5 – distinguishing between different types of historical change. However, it is a tricky idea and is best used as a basis for class discussion.

Activity: Note that the priest is sympathetic to the old Catholic ways of worship and decoration and that he has moved to Weaverham, described in Source 6, where other church members seem to think like him. He will be an old man now, with a lot to remember.

This activity could be done as an interview.

ENQUIRY: WERE THE CATHOLICS FRAMED?

Pupils' Book pp. 36–39

The Gunpowder Plot is one bit of history that most children learn from an early age and will have covered in Key Stage 2. Source 1 on page 36 is the version of it that most people still believe. This two-spread enquiry is orientated towards ATs 2 and 3 as pupils use a wide range of evidence to investigate other possible interpretations – specifically, the theory that the whole plot was set up by the government to discredit the Catholics in order to sanction more repressive measures against them.

The enquiry, therefore, follows on well from the earlier ones on the English Reformation, since it shows how disputes about religion were far from settled at the beginning of the seventeenth century. Indeed, they were destined to be a major factor in causing the Civil War.

(Pages 36–37)

Q1–3: AT3 levels 3, 5
Q4: AT3 levels 3, 4
Q5: AT1b levels 2, 3, AT3 level 3
Q6: AT1b level 2, AT3 level 3
Q7–8: AT3 levels 3, 4, 5, 7

Source 1: *Little Arthur's History of England* must rank as one of the most successful children's history books ever. It was still in print 150 years after first publication, and approaching its 100th edition.

You might do well to have other textbooks handy to refer to, which give similar versions of the story.

Question 3: You can suggest words for pupils to choose from: trustworthy, angry, suspicious, sad.

Question 4: Pupils will easily spot the modern anachronisms in Source 4 – the car, the TV aerial, etc. They will need to refer to the sources to spot some inaccuracies, such as the cellar not running under the Houses of Parliament.

(Pages 38–39)

Q1: AT3 levels 1, 3
Q2, 4: AT3 levels 1, 3, 5, 7
Q3: AT3 levels 3, 4, 5, 7
Q5: AT2 levels 2, 4, 5, 6, 7
Activity: AT2 levels 2, 3, 4, 5, 6, 7, 8, 9, 10, AT3 levels 3, 4, 5, 6, 7, 8

Activity: The closing speech should include for the prosecution:
■ a description of the crime
■ why it was an awful crime
■ why the plotters should be found guilty
■ how they should be punished.
For the defence:
■ a description of how the government planned the whole thing
■ how Guy Fawkes and the other 'plotters' were really victims in all this – the real blame lies elsewhere
■ how untrustworthy the evidence brought to the court is
■ how important it is for future relationships between the government and the Catholics that the plotters are treated mercifully.

Once the speeches are written, some of them could be read out, with the class in role. You can organise the classroom as in the illustration. The defence is on the left, the prosecution on the right, the jury in front of the dock.

ENQUIRY: WHAT DID ELIZABETH LOOK LIKE?

Pupils' Book pp. 40–41
Worksheet 6

'Packaging' of political leaders is something we take for granted today. But the Tudors did it too.

This one-spread enquiry picks up ideas described by Roy Strong of the National Portrait Gallery in his *Portraits of Queen Elizabeth I* (Oxford). These portraits were consciously used to 'package' Elizabeth – to project the desired image of the Queen to her people.

It is a wide ranging enquiry, embracing areas of AT1, AT2 and AT3.

Q1: AT1b level 2
Q2: AT1c level 2
Q3–4: AT3 levels 3, 4
Q5: AT1c level 6
Q6: AT3 levels 5, 6, 7
Q7: AT2 levels 2, 3, 8, 9, AT3 levels 3, 4
Q8: AT2 level 3
Activity: AT1b level 2, AT1c levels 4, 5, 6, 7

Questions 1 and 2 are for class discussion. Pupils should include newspapers, TV and radio, etc. They will hopefully also include touring the country. For Elizabeth, however, even this was problematic. The map below shows the extent of her travels around the country. In her 45-year reign she never travelled beyond the dotted line.

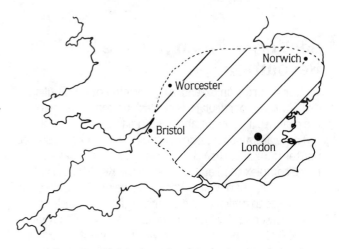

Question 3: Source 1 = B; Source 2 = A; Source 3 = E; Source 4 = C; Source 5 = G; Source 6 = F; Source 7 = H; Source 8 = D.

Worksheet 6 shows one method by which the official portraits were probably disseminated. It provides a 'pin prick' template for pupils to try their own hand at drawing a portrait of Elizabeth, along with a suggested colour scheme.

As an extension to question 5 you could display pupils' portraits and have a class vote on which Elizabeth would be most pleased with.

This is not the only example of Tudor 'propaganda'. We can see the Tudor interpretation of history in Shakespeare's history plays, most famously in *Richard III*.

Richard III, of course, was deposed and killed by Henry VII to found the Tudor dynasty. The Tudors' legitimacy depended to some extent on showing that this was a just deposition. Richard III is therefore shown to be unfit to rule. He is the only Shakespearian character who from the start of the play effectively announces to the audience that he is a villain. Then during the play he murders or executes everyone – including family and friends – who stands in the way of his becoming king. But when he finally faces up to his greatest enemy, Henry Tudor, he is defeated. Henry promises that peace, prosperity and order will now be established. It is a version of Richard that must have pleased Elizabeth and her court greatly and one which most people still believe today.

There might be a possibility of some cross-curricular work with the English department.

Question 7 approaches various levels of AT2. Pupils might better appreciate the Source 8 view of Elizabeth when they have studied the problems facing England in the 1620s which are investigated on the next page.

Question 8: This is getting at the difference between fact and opinion (AT2 level 3). It is best to set this as homework (they will have to do a little research) and then compare answers at the beginning of the next lesson.

Pupils can then try to create a set of statements of fact based on this spread and a second set of statements of opinion that they can all agree about.

Section 4: When was the English Revolution?

Section 4 forms an extended exploration of the English Civil War – in particular, its causes and consequences and the changes it brought about in England.

There are nine enquiries. Some of these present subject matter unfamiliar to Y8 and look at concepts that appear more complex than any covered in the Key Stage 3 core units so far. There will be choices to be made within each enquiry as to which of the exercises should be tackled.

The first enquiry looks at the causes of the Civil War, the next three investigate the war itself and its effect on ordinary people, and finally five enquiries look at the long- and short-term consequences of the Civil War.

ENQUIRY: WHY DID CIVIL WAR BREAK OUT IN 1642?

Pupils' Book pp. 42–49
Worksheet 7

'The causes of the Civil War' is a complex and difficult subject to expect twelve-year-olds to consider. So one aim in this enquiry has been to give a clear structure to the causes. We characterise them as four stages to war (which are the long-term causes) and six triggers (short-term causes), as summarised on the timeline on page 42.

However, this structure might easily give the mistaken impression that from an early point civil war was somehow inevitable. So our second aim has been to

underpin the enquiry with the question 'When did war become inevitable?' and to help pupils see that war was still an unlikely outcome of the arguments between King and Parliament until well into 1641.

This enquiry covers a major section of the Programme of Study, and allows pupils access to a wide range of ideas in AT1 strand b.

A lot of the material in it is ideal for class discussion and the teacher will have a crucial role in keeping up the momentum throughout the enquiry. There are various strategies you might employ during the course of the unit to help the various elements hang together.

Pupils might be asked to build up a cartoon strip, with one frame for each stage and trigger (using **Worksheet 7**), or to characterise each stage and trigger by a headline and a four-line description as we have done with some of the events on page 46.

Another approach is to divide the class into four groups and ask each group to investigate and report back on one of Stages 1–4. The story could then be built up as each group reported back. After each report you could ask 'Did these developments make the Civil War inevitable?'

You could also have large sheets of paper displayed around the wall of the classroom, one colour for Stages 1–4 and another for Triggers 1–6, and as the story progresses display work relating to that stage on its appropriate sheet.

(Pages 42–43)

The background: King and Parliament

The relationship between the monarch and Parliament had not been easy in either Elizabeth's or James' reign. Elizabeth called very few Parliaments: fifteen in the first 30 years of her reign. In James' reign it met twelve years out of 22. In the first fifteen years of Charles' reign it met for five years.

Stage 1: Charles I's reign gets off to bad start

Worksheet 13, *Was Charles a good king?*, will return to some of Charles' major decisions and actions and assess whether he made right or wrong decisions. It is designed to be used after page 58 of the pupils' book, as part of the study of the trial of Charles.

Stage 2: Charles rules without Parliament

Q1: AT3 levels 3, 4, 5

The class could be split into study groups to look at either money or religion – in which case use questions 5 and 6 on page 45 as summary questions for class discussion.

(Pages 44–45)

Q1: AT1b level 2, AT1c levels 6, 7
Q2: AT1c level 6, AT3 level 3
Q3–4: AT2 levels 7, 8
Q5–6: AT1b levels 4, 5, 6, 7, AT1c levels 4, 5

Question 1: Draw pupils' attention to the labelled features in Sources 6 and 7. They may need to refer back to the two churches shown in the reconstructions on pages 26 and 31.

Source 8 is from a Puritan pamphlet. Do some detailed interrogation of this visual in class. Who do pupils think are shown with Charles cutting down the tree? The person in the barrel, which should have been filled with the fruit of religion, has skewered the Prayer Book, the Bible (and a Puritan hat?) onto his pike. In the background the tree roots are being burned, while at the top whole branches are lopped off. Is the central figure poisoning the tree? God's sword points in judgement.

Source 11: Clarendon is key figure in the writing of Civil War history. He was a lawyer, and before the Civil War he was an MP in both the Short and the Long Parliaments. To start with he sided with the King's opponents, but as a strong churchman he began to side with the King once reform of the Church of England became an issue. He then became one of the King's chief supporters and advisers. After the war he joined Charles' son in exile, and returned with him at the Restoration in 1660 to become chief minister to Charles II, a position he held until 1667 when he fell out of favour.

Question 6: The same question is asked again at two strategic points, on page 47 (summer 1641) and page 49 (June 1642).

Stage 3: The Scots rebel against the new Prayer Book

Activity: AT1c levels 4, 5, AT3 levels 1, 3

Pupils might need reminding that James I (Charles' father) had become King of England as well as Scotland on Elizabeth's death. We don't deal with these events until our survey of the uniting of the kingdom on page 72. However, an awareness of the differences between Scotland and England is an important part of appreciating Britain's regional diversity, and helps set up the later enquiry on the Jacobites (page 74).

(Pages 46–47)

Q1: AT1b levels 4, 5, 6

Stage 4: The Long Parliament demands reform

Q1: AT3 levels 1, 3, 4
Q2–3: AT1c levels 4, 5, 6, AT3 level 3
Q4: AT1b levels 4, 6, 7, AT1c levels 4, 5

Question 1: The demands and concessions in Sources 13 and 14 could be written on individual coloured cards, and then matched by groups of pupils working together. You may find it easier to number the statements.

Parliament had its way in everything bar the reversal of the reforms of the Church of England. Pupils will soon see how it was religious differences which finally began to divide the House of Commons into supporters and opponents of the King.

Trigger 1: November 1641: the Grand Remonstrance

This is a crucial transition. You will need to emphasise the consensus that in June 1641 war did not seem inevitable. From now on we are into the short-term causes and triggers which changed that situation.

Call attention to the closeness of the vote.

Trigger 2: November 1642: the Irish Rebellion

Q1: AT1b level 2, AT1c level 6

(Pages 48–49)

Trigger 3: January 1642: Charles tries to arrest five MPs

Q1–3: AT3 levels 3, 4, 5, 6, 7
Q4: AT1b level 2, AT1c levels 6, 7

Question 1: Interrogate Source 16 in detail in preparation for question 1. Which is Charles, which the Speaker? What attitudes do the various MPs seem to have to Charles – suspicious, approving, afraid, angry?

Then move on to interrogate Source 17. In particular, what does the Speaker's speech mean?

One of the main differences, obviously, is that Charles has no soldiers with him in Source 16. He looks like a lone crusader or a noble statesman. The MPs look decidedly shifty and cowed.

Question 3: Point out to pupils the information in the two source lines. In the case of Source 17 note particularly that he was an eye-witness, took shorthand notes and as a clerk would be trained in recording proceedings accurately.

Trigger 4: February 1642: religious divisions

We have already come across Clarendon as an example of an MP who changed sides for religious reasons.

Trigger 6: 1 June 1642: the Commons go too far

Q1: AT1b level 2, AT1c levels 6, 7
Q2: AT1b levels 4, 6, 7, AT1c levels 4, 5

Summary Q1: AT1b levels 3, 4, 5
Summary Q2: AT1b level 5
Summary Q3–4: AT1b level 6
Summary Q5: AT1b levels 6, 7, 8, 9
Activity: AT1b levels 2, 3, 4, 5, 6, 7, 8, 9, AT1c levels 6, 7

Summary questions 1–5: A set of causation questions that build on one another.

Question 1: Groups may need a lot of guidance. Their lists should begin with the four stages and the six triggers. They could then add to the list other events or developments that they think are significant.

Question 2: Once the list is complete each member of the group could categorise a few of the causes, or the categorisation could be a group decision.

Their lists should at least include (although with many of them there is scope for debate):

- Charles marries Henrietta Maria (R, P)
- Charles makes Buckingham, who is unpopular with Parliament, his chief minister (P)
- Charles rules without Parliament for eleven years (P)
- Raising Ship Money (M)
- Laud's reforms (R)
- Punishing Puritan leaders (R)
- Extending Laud reforms to Scotland (R)
- Suspicion of Strafford (P)
- Charles dismisses Short Parliament (P)
- Scotland and England go to war (R, P)
- The long Parliament demands reforms (R, M, P)
- The Grand remonstrance (R, P)
- The Irish Rebellion (R)
- The attempted arrest of the MPs (P)
- Arguments about religion (R)
- Arguments about control of the army (P)
- The Nineteen Propositions (R, M, P)
- Charles raises his standard (P)

Questions 3, 4 and 5: Before tackling these have a class discussion around pupils' lists of causes and the way they have categorised them. Questions 3, 4 and 5 could then be a continuation of the class discussion.

Activity: This expands question 5. It accesses levels 2–9 of AT1b. Use the posters to make a class display.

ENQUIRY: WHO FOUGHT WHOM?

Pupils' Book pp. 50–51
Worksheet 8

A single-spread enquiry that emphasises work on AT3 as pupils firstly compare traditional descriptions of how English Civil War loyalties were determined against some primary and secondary sources on the subject and secondly compare the equipment of the two sides' soldiers.

Q1, 3: AT3 levels 3, 4
Q2: AT3 level 7

It was true that the ordinary people did not usually choose who to support. However, the gentry usually did choose. There are examples of divided families, e.g. the Feildings of Denbigh, where father and son decided to fight on different sides.

And in choosing sides ideology was not always the only determinant of loyalty. There is evidence that people aimed to back the winner. Cory Gardiner (MP) went so far as to say, 'The World now accounts it policy for the father to be on one side and the son on the other.' This may be one explanation for why people changed sides during the war as well.

It would be ideal in this context to introduce a few local examples. What were your town's loyalties during the war? What about neighbouring towns? Were there any famous individuals fighting on either side?

Question 1: Discuss Source 4, which is quite densely packed with information, before attempting questions 1 and 2.

Question 3: Support can be offered by giving pupils a list of six statements from which they have to pick three.

The soldiers

Q1: AT3 levels 3, 4
Q2: AT1b level 2, AT3 level 3

Source 7: This is a Royalist window, made in 1660 on the restoration of the monarchy, in memory of the Cheshire gentlemen who served for the King. Around the outside are the gentlemen with their coats of arms. In the centre are various weapons and pieces of armour. See how many pupils can spot. In the top half there is a musket, a musket stand, a powder belt, a baton, a spur, two breastplates, two helmets, neck armour, and a pike. In the lower half, two pikes, two swords, another pike, a whistle, a drum and drumsticks, and a standard.

Question 1: Worksheet 8 is an outline drawing of Sources 6 and 8. Make a copy for each pupil.

ENQUIRY: WHAT WAS LIFE LIKE DURING THE CIVIL WAR?

Pupils' Book pp. 52–55
Worksheets 9, 10, 12

In this two-spread enquiry we have provided three separate case studies which give differing perspectives on what life was like in the Civil War. A wide range of evidence is used – a nineteenth-century painting, a collection of letters from the Civil War period and a range of prints, cartoons and contemporary descriptions. Together the case studies access ATs 1, 2 and 3.

Many other case studies could be used and, in particular, you may have local stories or case studies you can introduce – check with your local museum or castle, or local history society.

There may well be starting points for this unit in the current news bulletins. Civil war is a common phenomenon: there are ample demonstrations that civil wars are among the bloodiest and most cruel of human conflicts.

(Pages 52–53)
Case study 1: When did you last see your father?

Activity: AT1b level 2, AT1c level 6, AT3 level 3

Source 1: Painted in 1878 by William Frederick Yeames.

Activity: Once pupils have worked out their ideas about the story behind the painting they could present it in drama or mime and include what might happen next.

Case study 2: Lady Harley defends her castle

Activity: AT3 level 1

Worksheet 9 (a version of Source 3) and **Worksheet 10** (a template for breaking the code) can together be used to present this letter in a more realistic way. The second letter on Worksheet 9 is printed without distinguishing the code words. Some pupils might like the challenge of trying to decipher this other letter – first of all with no clues given at all as to where the message words are, i.e. as an enemy soldier intercepting it might find it, then using the template on Worksheet 10.

Sources 4 and 5: The conclusion of the story is told through the eyes of another resident of the castle, not through Lady Harley's own words.

(Pages 54–55)

Q1–3: AT3 levels 1, 3
Q4: AT3 levels 3, 4
Activity: AT1c levels 6, 7, AT2 levels 2, 3

The siege was the typical form of engagement of the Civil War. **Worksheet 12** – which can be used here or after the enquiry on Marston Moor – examines a military record made by Thomas Fairfax, Parliamentary commander, showing what his army did between April and October 1645. It allows pupils to see that the Civil War was much more typically a war of sieges than a war of open pitched battles.

Case study 3: 'Plunder and violence'

Q1–2: AT3 levels 1, 3, 4
Q3: AT1c levels 6, 7, AT3 level 3
Q4: AT3 levels 3, 4, 7
Activity: AT1c levels 6, 7, AT2 levels 6, 7

Source 9: Notice that in the background Birmingham is shown burning, which allows comparison with Source 7.

Question 3: Pupils can tackle the question using just two or three sources, e.g. Sources 9, 11 and 13.

Pupils' explanation of their choice is very important. They will need to interrogate the source lines as well as the sources themselves. They might, for example, think Source 9 is a glorification of Prince Rupert, but the title of the pamphlet suggests it was actually a pamphlet against him.

Source 10 might appear to be condemning the Parliamentarian soldiers; however, the original caption to this print reads 'The soldiers in their passage to York turn unto reformers, pull down Popish pictures, break down rayles and turn altars into tables.' In other words, the picture is pro-Parliamentarian.

Sources 7, 8, 9, 10, 11 and 12 were produced by Parliamentarians, Source 13 by neutrals. None of the sources were produced by Royalists.

Question 4: This could be tackled using just Source 12 or just Source 13.

Activity: You could have some pamphlets to hand. They usually had long and exotic titles and an evocative cartoon, such as the ones below.

◆▬◆▬◆▬◆▬◆▬◆▬◆▬◆▬◆▬◆▬◆▬◆▬◆▬◆▬◆

ENQUIRY: WHY DID THE ROYALISTS LOSE AT MARSTON MOOR?

Pupils' Book pp. 56–57
Worksheets 11, 12

In the early years of the Civil War it was the Royalist troops who were better equipped, better led and better trained. They achieved many military successes to prove it, but failed to deliver the knock-out blow. It was not until around 1644 that the Parliamentarians began to rival them in military skill.

This single-spread enquiry examines a strategic battle of the Civil War when the balance of power decisively shifted. It dented for the first time the King's strong support in the north of England. It allowed Cromwell to emerge as the most influential Parliamentary leader.

The Royalists did not lose the Civil War at Marston Moor, but they never again looked as if they could win it.

The enquiry focuses on AT1b as it considers the reasons for the Royalists' defeat and AT3 as it studies a range of primary and secondary accounts of the battle to piece together what actually happened.

The battle

Q1: AT3 levels 3, 4
Q2: AT3 level 1
Q3: AT3 level 3
Q4: AT1b levels 4, 5, 6, 7, 8

Worksheet 11 is a photocopiable blank with two plans of the Marston Moor battle site for pupils to use in answering question 1.

Question 4: For this question you should point out to the pupils the vagueness of Charles' instructions to Rupert. He failed to make it clear whether he wanted Rupert just to save York or also to defeat the Parliamentary armies.

Worksheet 12 about the actions of Thomas Fairfax's army in 1645 can be used here to give a more complete picture of the style of military engagement that typified the Civil War.

ENQUIRY: WHY DID THE ENGLISH EXECUTE THEIR KING?

Pupils' Book pp. 58–61
Worksheets 13, 14

The trial and execution of Charles I form a watershed in British political history, and accordingly in this unit. England no longer had a monarch or a monarchy. Was this the English Revolution: the decisive change?

The aim of this two-spread enquiry is to give a feel for what went on at Charles' trial: to show what arguments were used for and against him, and to demonstrate how

cautious even some of his opponents were about going all the way and putting him on trial for treason. There is clear evidence that Charles won the argument, but his opponents were determined to get rid of him in any case. What else could they do? If they let him continue to rule they would have fought two costly wars for nothing.

We will investigate a range of ideas in AT1 strands b and c as we try to find out why people acted as they did, and what the range of attitudes to the trial and execution was.

There are direct comparisons to be made with the trial of Louis XVI 144 years later. This indeed is the point of the word 'English' in the enquiry title: to set up a comparison with the trial of Louis on page 128. The same dilemma confronted the French revolutionaries – they had effectively gained power, but what were they now to do with the King?

Worksheet 13, *Was Charles a good king?* can be used to introduce this spread and to help pupils form an overall view of Charles' actions.

The actions that Charles actually took were 1b) (page 42), 2a) (page 42), 3b) (page 43), 4a) (page 45), 5b) (page 46), 6c) (page 47), 7b) (page 48), 8a) (page 58).

(Pages 58–59)

The first day: Saturday 20 January 1649

Q1: AT3 level 3
Q2: AT3 levels 3, 4

The second day: Monday 22 January

It might be worthwhile to point out that the trial started on a Saturday. Sunday was of course a rest day for Puritans – thus the Monday was the second day of the trial.

The third day: Tuesday 23 January

Q1: AT3 level 3

(Pages 60–61)

Verdict and sentence

Q1: AT1c levels 4, 6, 7
Activity: AT1b levels 3, 4, 5, 6, 7, AT1c levels 4, 5, 6, 7, 8, AT3 levels 3, 4

Activity: Lay out the classroom like a court – see Source 4.

Depending on your own skills and the abilities of your class you might consider whether to:
■ play Charles yourself
■ get another teacher or a visitor to play Bradshaw
■ brief some pupils separately as judges.

The key to making the most of this role-play opportunity is in the preparation. Each pupil or group of pupils should decide on one main argument they can use against Charles, and one main argument they can use in his defence.

In addition, **Worksheet 14** gives some cue cards to copy and hand out to pupils to help prime them as witnesses for and against Charles. There are three witnesses for the prosecution, three for the defence, and an additional role – the neutral – who can be called to help the court in its deliberations.

Execution: Tuesday 30 January

Q1–2: AT3 levels 1, 3
Q3: AT3 levels 3, 4
Q4: AT1b level 2
Q5: AT3 levels 4, 5, 6, 7, 9
Q6: AT1b levels 6, 7

Question 1: The scene on the scaffold shows three moments in the execution: Charles takes off his coat, Charles is beheaded, Charles' head is held up.

Question 5: The emphasis in this question is on the idea that sources can give reliable evidence of some things while not of others, an idea in AT3 level 9.

ENQUIRY: CHARLES THE MARTYR OR CHARLES THE TRAITOR?

Pupils' Book pp. 62–63
Worksheet 15

This single-spread enquiry focuses on ideas within AT2. It looks at the rewriting of history that began almost the moment Charles had died.

Rewriting history

Q1: AT3 level 3
Activity 1: AT2 levels 2, 3, 4, 5, 6, 7, 8, 9
Activity 2: AT1c levels 4, 5, 6, 7

Eikon Basilike means Royal Image. The book was subtitled *The Portraiture of his Sacred Majestie in his Solitudes and Sufferings*. It purported to be meditations written by Charles himself. It was wildly popular and went into 47 editions in a few months. Parliament decided to commission a reply, written by John Milton, which attempted to refute it paragraph by paragraph.

Charles became a symbol for all those who wished to support the idea of monarchy, who wanted to resist the trend towards rule by the army, and who wanted to preserve the Church of England.

The 'Charles the Martyr' lobby prospered. There was an official feast day in the Anglican Church calendar for Charles the Martyr until 1859, and the Society of King

Charles the Martyr is still campaigning for the reintroduction of this feast day. The SKCM is only one of three Charles I societies that still lay wreaths at the site of Charles' execution in Whitehall every year on 30 January. The story continues!

Activity 2: This activity is best done in groups, where pupils can brainstorm ideas first. You could show them an application form used today, e.g. for a teacher's job.

When you discuss their ideas for forms the points to look out for are character, family background, religion (and religion of wife), children (heirs), etc. You might find some of the forms are anachronistic, in that they look for twentieth-century attitudes and abilities. This could lead to a useful class discussion.

After pupils have made their application forms, but before they have filled them in for Charles, take a photocopy which will be kept and then filled in for Cromwell as part of the next enquiry. This will allow a comparison between Charles and Cromwell. The same form can also be used for Louis XVI of France.

Worksheet 15 is a support worksheet that provides an application form for pupils to base their ideas on or to use instead of making their own application form.

ENQUIRY: WHAT KIND OF MAN WAS OLIVER CROMWELL?

Pupils' Book pp. 64–67
Worksheets 15, 16

The King's execution was one of the most obvious consequences of the Civil War. In the next three enquiries we study a range of other consequences.

First of all we investigate Cromwell and try to interpret his actions at a number of key moments between 1649 and 1658. We see how the evidence can be used to give differing interpretations of Cromwell's ambitions.

(Pages 64–65)

Pupils may well need some help in picturing the situation in England in 1649 – without a king for the first time. You could draw parallels with a school without teachers: who might take over? The strongest, the cleverest, etc...?

The army was the only effective ruling force, much as it is in many countries around the world today. It was certainly more powerful than Parliament: this was amply illustrated when Cromwell used the army to prevent MPs who were opposed to Charles' trial from attending Parliament.

The Irish Rebellion

Q1–4: AT3 levels 3, 4
Q5: AT3 level 7
Q6: AT2 levels 3, 4, 5, 6, 7, 8, 9, 10

This event will be picked up again on page 73 in the context of changing relationships between Ireland and England.

Questions 1–6 are best used for class discussion.

Question 5: Use a grid to analyse the answers.

Question 6: There will be disagreement about whether Cromwell's actions were justified, which will enable you to raise AT2 issues about why these different interpretations exist.

Cromwell and Parliament

Q1: AT3 level 3
Q2: AT1b level 2, AT1c level 3

Source 7: The words in the centre read: 'Begone you rogues you have sat long enough.'

(Pages 66–67)

The Lord Protector

Q1: AT3 levels 1, 3
Q2: AT2 levels 2, 8, AT3 levels 3, 4
Q3: AT1c level 4, AT2 level 7

Question 1: For class discussion. The cartoon is entitled Cromwell's Chariot or Cromwell's Car. It is full of symbols:

■ Cromwell is riding in the chariot. He has wolf's legs and hands.

■ The Devil is driving the chariot.

■ The King has been run over – turn the page upside down and it's more obviously a likeness – as well as a symbolic figure representing Justice. Cromwell has taken Justice's scales and balanced them on his sword.

■ The weeping women represent England, Scotland and Ireland – all at Cromwell's mercy. They are weeping as Cromwell grabs England's crown.

■ In the background wolves are chasing a flock of sheep and a hawk is preparing to pounce on a dove.

Source 11 presents opportunities for citizenship education. Pupils might like to compare this Protectorate with our present-day government. Draw a comparable diagram on the board and invite pupils to suggest how to fill in each area in a class discussion.

The 'king'?

Q1: AT3 level 1
Activity: AT1c levels 4, 5, 6, 7, AT2 levels 6, 7, 8, AT3 level 10

Activity: Worksheet 16 gives a blank newspaper front page which can be blown up to A3 for pupils to use in this activity. Encourage them to use word processors or DTP (if available) to present their articles.

This could be developed into a major piece of work, using additional books and visuals for pupils to research background material on Cromwell, his opinions, his career before and during the Civil War, and judgements on him by other commentators.

You could also fill out the King's application form (Worksheet 15) for Cromwell and compare his qualifications with Charles'.

Worksheet 40 invites comparisons between Cromwell and Napoleon and will be used after page 163 of Unit B (see page 86 of these notes).

ENQUIRY: THE WORLD TURNED UPSIDE DOWN

Pupils' Book pp. 68–69

This single-spread enquiry investigates one of the most obvious changes brought about by the English Civil War: the abundance of new political and religious ideas that flourished in its wake.

To help establish from the start the shock of radical ideas you could introduce the lesson by writing on the board or announcing to the pupils a number of fairly radical statements about society, wealth or the family that might be heard today and which most pupils would feel strongly about and preferably *disagree* with. The kind of statements you choose will be determined by the background of your pupils. Statements such as 'Only the rich should pay tax', 'A woman's place is in the home', or 'Britain is a racist society' might suit a range of contexts.

Women try to be heard

Q1: AT1c level 6, AT3 level 3
Q2: AT1c level 2
Q3: AT3 levels 3, 4

The Levellers

Q1: AT1c levels 2, 4, 6
Q2: AT1c levels 4, 5, 6, 7, 8, 9
Q3: AT3 levels 1, 3
Q4: AT3 level 3
Activity: AT1a levels 3, 4, AT1b levels 2, 3, 4, AT1c levels 4, 5, 6, 7

Questions 1 and 2: Both intended for class discussion.

Question 1: Pupils may need a lot of help on whether such ideas are acceptable today. It is best to begin by listing all the ideas, then splitting them into two lists. You could make this a small group activity by giving each group of pupils one of the radical ideas or movements to focus on.

These questions raise a number of citizenship issues, especially to do with equality of opportunity and the rights of minorities. The ideal of equality – as Margaret Thatcher was so keen to remind us – was not invented by

◆◆◆◆◆◆◆◆◆◆◆◆◆◆◆◆◆◆◆◆◆◆◆◆◆◆◆◆◆◆◆

the French Revolution, although she didn't cite the Diggers or Levellers in her argument. Pupils will have seen Winstanley's critique of the Magna Carta in their study of the latter in *Contrasts and Connections* (Source 4 on page 137).

Activity: A deceptively simple idea that allows pupils to cover ideas across all strands of AT1. For support work you might suggest that some pupils choose between two groups only, e.g. the Diggers and the women.

ENQUIRY: JAMES II – THE SAME OLD STORY?

Pupils' Book pp. 70–71
Worksheet 17

This one-spread enquiry rounds off Section 4 by looking at the Glorious Revolution and the changed relationship between king and Parliament that it demonstrated.

You will need to begin this spread by using the timeline (Worksheet 1 and page 1 of the pupils' book) and the mini-timeline at the top of the page to establish that we have moved on a number of decades from the Civil War. Otherwise there is a risk that pupils may confuse the Glorious Revolution with the Civil War.

Q1–3: AT1b level 2, AT1c level 6
Q4: AT3 level 3

The harsh punishment of the Monmouth rebels is infamous. They were first choked for a few minutes at the end of a rope. Their clothes were then cut off, their bellies slit open and their entrails burnt on a fire nearby. The remainder of the corpse was quartered and boiled in tar. The limbs and head were set on pikes on the roadside. It took many days to deal with all 250.

King and Parliament

Activity: AT1a levels 3, 4, 5, 6, 7

Source 3 is an attempt to demonstrate the changed relationship visually: the monarch, from being aloof and powerful, has been tied down by a series of changes.

Activity: For support you might like to give the pupils suggestions for changes resulting from the Civil War so that they simply decide which list to put them in. For example:
- England no longer had a king.
- New radical ideas spread.
- The army became the most powerful force in England.
- The king's powers were reduced.
- Catholicism was very unpopular.
- Ireland was brutally treated.
- Parliament's powers were increased.
- People were free to worship as they liked.
- England had a Lord Protector instead of a king.
- Charles I was seen as a martyr.

Section 5: How modern was the United Kingdom?

In the next four enquiries we shall be looking for evidence that the United Kingdom, during the period 1500–1750, became something recognisably more modern, more like the UK we live in today. We use political, social and scientific case studies.

We take as our starting point the element of the Programme of Study that deals with the process of increasing political unification, and survey the changes during the period which created the political entity we call the UK. Against that background, in the second enquiry, we examine the Jacobite Rebellion of 1745 to see if there are signs here that the political union was weak or strong, popular or unpopular, as far as Scotland was concerned.

The third enquiry is more self-contained. It looks at the Scientific Revolution and investigates how far scientific and technological developments had transformed everyday aspects of life in the England of the 1700s.

Finally, we focus on London and the changes that took place during the period in the UK's capital city.

ENQUIRY: UNITING THE KINGDOM

Pupils' Book pp. 72–73
Worksheet 18

A single-spread enquiry, which gives an overview of the key events between 1500 and 1750 that changed the relationships between the nations of the British Isles.

Q1: AT1c level 4
Q2–3: AT1a levels 3, 4, 5, AT1b levels 3, 4, 5, 6
Q4: AT1a level 3, AT1c level 4
Q5: AT1a levels 1, 3, 4

Question 1: Worksheet 18 provides a map to be used for this exercise. The labels are supposed to be very simple – just one or two words for each country.

Questions 2 and 3: Pupils could do one or the other in pairs or groups. In which case question 4 is for class discussion based on their findings.

Question 5: Source 3 is 1603, Source 4 is 1543, Source 5 is 1707.

ENQUIRY: HOW UNITED WAS THE UNITED KINGDOM?

Pupils' Book pp. 74–77
Worksheet 19

Not only is the Jacobite Rebellion of 1745 a very good story, it also helps throw light on the relationship between Scotland and England. In this two-spread enquiry we use it as a case study to help us answer the question 'How united was the United Kingdom?'.

Two main questions are posed:
■ Was the rebellion evidence that the Scots were dissatisfied with the union?
■ Why is Bonnie Prince Charlie such a romantic figure to so many people?

The starting point for this work could be to look at demands for devolution and independence in Scotland (as at the time of writing) or elsewhere.

(Pages 74–75)

Q1: AT1c level 4, AT3 levels 1, 3

Question 1: This could be attempted at several levels: as a straightforward reading of a family tree, or from the point of view of a Protestant or of a Catholic.

The background

Q1–2: AT1b levels 2, 3, 4, 5

Questions 1 and 2: For class discussion.
   Source 5: This shows Charlie landing at Eriskay with his seven supporters. By the time he reached Glenfinnan he had over 200 men.

Gathering support

Q1: AT3 levels 1, 3
Q2: AT3 level 3

There are two useful documents which help us find out what kind of people supported the Jacobite Rebellion.
■ Soon after the rebellion a list was drawn up by local tax collectors of who had joined it. This list contains 2500 names – most of them from the Lowlands.
■ There is also a list of prisoners taken in the '45 Rebellion, which provides information about another 3500 of the rebels and contains much more information about the supporters from the Highlands.

Historians have analysed these lists and worked out a profile of the Jacobite supporters according to their occupations. The most common status was that of landowner, and the next most numerous categories were (in descending order) servants, farmers, labourers, merchants, workmen, brewers, shoemakers, lawyers.

Edinburgh

Q1: AT3 level 3

(Pages 76–77)

Into England

Pupils could be asked after reading Source 12 to consider what they would advise Charlie to do now, and why – as they are again in the next paragraph.

The retreat

Q1: AT1b levels 3, 4, 5, 6, 7, 8, 9

Question 1: This is the key question. You could follow it up by asking whether there is any evidence that Scotland as a whole wanted to leave the union.

After the rebellion

Q1–2: AT2 levels 2, 3, 4, 5, 6, 7, 8, 9
Activity: Many aspects of AT1, AT2 and AT3

Of the 3500 rebels mentioned in the List of Prisoners, 1200 were set free, 1000 were transported to become slaves in British colonies in America and the West Indies, 120 were executed and 200 were banished from Britain. There is no account of the rest, but it is thought they died from disease or from their wounds in prison.

The Jacobite story leads naturally into the story of the Highland Clearances, which is covered in the next core unit, **Expansion, Trade and Industry 1750–1900.**
   Activity: This is a very open-ended activity and, depending on how it is approached by the pupils, might embrace any of the strands of AT1 and open up profound possibilities for work towards ATs 2 and 3.

One group could be told to organise the programme as a 'hatchet job' on Charlie, another to do a 'whitewash'.
   Worksheet 19 is a 'programme running order' for the pupils to help structure their response.

Have other resource books and visuals available in class so that pupils can do further research if they want to.

ENQUIRY: SCIENCE AND SUPERSTITION

Pupils' Book pp. 78–91

One of the important ideas for pupils to grasp in AT1 strand a is that change is seldom uniform – changes move through a society at different rates for different people. One of the aims of this two-spread enquiry is for pupils to see that while the seventeenth century can be characterised as a time of scientific and technological improvement, it was also a time of increased superstition, as manifested by the growing witch craze. New ideas and new discoveries were spreading rapidly but superstitions were abounding too.

The enquiry raises the question 'How modern was the UK?'.

(Pages 78–79)

The Scientific Revolution

Activity: AT3 levels 1, 2, 3
Q1: AT1a levels 3, 5
Q2: AT1a levels 3, 4

Use the narrative to tell the story in your own way.

Source 1: This experiment was based on the ideas developed by Robert Boyle 100 years earlier to demonstrate the properties of air (see 1661 in the timeline on page 79).

Joseph Wright of Derby painted many such subjects, focusing among other things on science and industry. He had a meticulous eye for detail and his paintings were based on thorough research over a long period.

Activity: Pupils could develop a scene to act out based on this painting.

Source 5: You can do Harvey's experiment in class by following the instructions given in the diagram.

Questions 1 and 2: Best used for class discussion. Make sure pupils explain the reasons for their choice.

(Pages 80–81)

Case study 1: Medicine and health

Q1–2: AT3 levels 1, 3
Q3: AT1c level 2

Question 1: From the bottom left clockwise the scenes are: extracting a tooth, an amputation, letting blood (a common way of treating many ailments as doctors believed most diseases were caused by poison in the blood), inspecting urine, repairing a dislocated shoulder, checking for a breast tumour.

Question 2: The remaining scene (bottom right) might be saying goodbye to a healed patient, or dispensing drugs. In the centre panel the doctor is shown holding his doctor's diploma or certificate, with his drugs arrayed on shelves behind him.

Case study 2: The witch hunts

Q1: AT1c level 2
Q2: AT1b level 2, AT1c levels 4, 6
Activity: AT1c level 4

Keith Thomas, a leading historian on the witch hunts, has explained the sudden upsurge of court cases against witches as in part a response to the Reformation: 'Before the Reformation the Catholic Church had provided an elaborate ritual to ward off evil spirits. Someone who fell victim to witchcraft did not need to take his case to court. After the Reformation Protestant preachers denied that the old rituals (holy water, priests' prayers, the sign of the cross) had any effect. The only way out in these circumstances was to take the witch to court.'

Summary Q1: AT1a levels 3, 4, 5, 6, 7, AT1b levels 3, 4, 5, 6, 7, 8, 9, 10, AT1c levels 3, 4, 5, 6, 7, 8, 9, 10

This **Summary question** has very wide ranging possibilities within all strands of AT1, as well as opening up work towards a range of levels in AT3.

SOCIETIES IN CHANGE THE MAKING OF THE UK

It is best taken as a class discussion to start with. Draw up two columns on the board, one listing evidence to support the view that there was a scientific revolution in the seventeenth century and the other listing evidence to combat that view.

This enquiry will prove a useful basis for understanding the spread of new ideas that was a contributing factor in the French Revolution (see page 112 of Unit B).

ENQUIRY: HOW DID LONDON CHANGE?

Pupils' Book pp. 82–87
Worksheets 20, 21, 22

This enquiry reviews the whole period 1500–1750. By focusing on a single city over a long period it allows pupils to appreciate how change is usually a result of a range of different factors.

Social factors (such as the movement of people from the country to the city looking for work) and economic factors (such as the increasing international trade handled through London) combined with accidents (such as the Great Fire or the Plague) and technological developments (such as the printing methods that allowed the newspaper industry to grow) to bring about change in London.

Pupils should be able to build on their Key Stage 2 study of the Plague and the Great Fire of London.

(Pages 82–83)

London in the 1500s

Q1–2: AT1c level 4, AT3 levels 1, 3

Source 1: This can be interrogated in detail now, but the main work with this visual will be done in question 1 on page 86, when it will be compared with Source 12. There is an incredible amount of detail to be seen on both pictures.

Worksheet 20 is an outline drawing of Source 1 with an indication of the extent of London at various points during the Middle Ages and during the period 1500–1750. Mask off task B, which will be used later on (see page 42 below).

Question 1 should be done in class. We can see or surmise the following occupations: butchers, dicers (gamblers?), carters, fishmongers, timber-merchants, milk-sellers, honey-sellers, bakers, cordwainers (shoemakers), wine-merchants, rope-makers, steel-makers, oyster-catchers, fishermen, cooks, candle-makers, corn-merchants, poultry-sellers and various bankers and money-lenders (Jews and Lombards).

Question 2: Worksheet 21 has an outline drawing of Source 3 for pupils to annotate and describe.

The Plague

Q1–2, 6, 7: AT3 level 1
Q3: AT1c level 2
Q4–5: AT3 level 3

Question 1: The total of deaths shown is 5225.

Question 2: The three most common causes of death were: Plague 3880, fever 353 and spotted fever (which might be measles or scarlet fever) 190.

Questions 3 and 4: Pupils will quickly see that many of these are of course descriptions of symptoms, not diagnoses or causes of death.

Some definitions:

apoplexy – rupture of brain artery
chrisomes – babies who died before they were christened (less than a month old)
consumption – TB
convulsion – especially in infants
dropsy – fluid retention in tissues
fistula – ulcer
flux – diarrhoea or bleeding
King's evil – scrofula (like TB)
palsy – paralysis
quinsy – sore throat or tonsilitis
rickets – softening of bones (deficiency of Vitamin D)
rising of the lights – probably a pneumonic condition (lights = lungs)
scowring – diarrhoea
sote – drunk
purplis – a purple rash
starved at nurse – died with wet nurse
stone – gall or bladder stone
strangury – pain passing urine
surfeit – overeating.

Questions 6 and 7: In some classes you might want to give pupils only one or two dates from the diary extract to investigate.

(Pages 84–85)

Q1: AT3 levels 1, 3, 4
Q2: AT1c level 4, AT3 level 3
Activity: AT1c levels 2, 4, 5, 6

Question 1: Worksheet 22 is a copy of Source 7 for pupils to annotate.

Activity: the diagram opposite shows what actually caused the Plague.

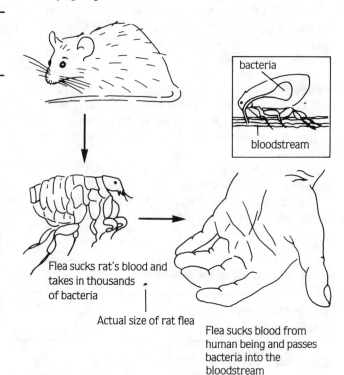

Rat carrying Plague bacteria

bacteria

bloodstream

Flea sucks rat's blood and takes in thousands of bacteria

Actual size of rat flea

Flea sucks blood from human being and passes bacteria into the bloodstream

The Great Fire of London: a blessing in disguise?

Q1: AT3 level 3
Q2: AT1b level 3

Question 1: Use **Worksheet 20** (with task A masked off) to mark where the artist was. B is correct.

(Pages 86–87)

London in the 1700s

Q1: AT1a level 3
Q2: AT1a level 3, AT1c level 4

Questions 1 and 2 are for class discussion.

Activity: AT1c level 4

London will be examined again in depth in the next British core unit – **Expansion, Trade and Industry** – when the growth of Britain's trade and Empire and its worldwide contacts will also be looked at in detail.

Section 6: Conclusion

ENQUIRY: A TOUR AROUND BRITAIN

Pupils' Book pp. 88–93
Worksheet 23

This concluding enquiry gives a picture of the United Kingdom in the mid-eighteenth century. The five journeys take in all corners of the country and give a picture of agriculture, industry, jobs, cities, towns, villages, houses and people. They will help pupils to appreciate some of the regional diversity of the country and some of the changes that had come about since 1500.

The enquiry lays the foundations for both a local study in the summer term of Y8 and Expansion, Trade and Industry in Y9. It also provides a point of comparison with France in the mid-eighteenth century, on the eve of the Revolution, which will be examined at the start of the next unit.

(Pages 88–89)

Source 1: One of the important changes in Britain which underlies many of the features being observed is population growth (see graph below). Between 1500 and 1750 the population of England trebled.

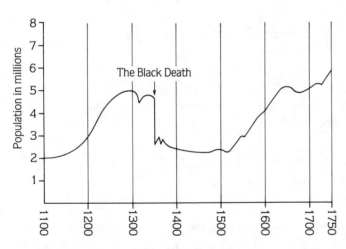

Worksheet 23 is a map for pupils to use throughout this enquiry to mark the places Defoe visited (see also question 1 on page 93).

Journey 1: East Anglia

Q1–2: AT3 levels 1, 3, 4

These questions are designed for class discussion, as are the majority of questions in this enquiry.

Journey 2: the South West

Q1: AT1c level 4, AT3 level 3

Source 8: You will need to interrogate this in detail. Notice the following: cheese fair, joiners' and turners' (carpentry) wares, leather fair, basketmen's fair, horse fair, sheep fair, hops (for beer making) fair.

SOCIETIES IN CHANGE THE MAKING OF THE UK

(Pages 90–91)

Journey 3: the West and Wales

Q1–2: AT3 level 3
Q3: AT3 levels 1, 3

Question 1: Notice: unloading bales of cotton, various forms of transport (ships, a carriage, a horse-drawn 'sledge', packhorses), children on a home-made see-saw, a woman carrying a basket on her head. Notice the street lights as well.

Question 2: Source 11 is from a frontispiece to a book. It shows shearing, weaving, shipbuilding, farming, mining, forestry, fishing (anti-clockwise from top right).

Journey 4: the North

Q1–3: AT3 levels 1, 2, 3

Question 1: The cloth market is in the main street just up from the bridge.

Question 2: Street names give evidence of dyers, millers and pig keeping (Swine Gate and Boar Lane); boats on rivers and warehouses show importance of warehousemen, labourers and transport workers; the houses around the outside are mostly of merchants.

Question 3: There are three Anglican churches (St John's (already seen in Source 7 on page 44), Trinity and St Peter's. There is a Presbyterian meeting house on the left, a Quaker meeting house bottom left and a Free Church meeting house in the centre in Gall Lane.

(Pages 92–93)

Q1–2: AT3 level 3

Journey 5: the Highlands and Islands

Q1–3: AT3 levels 1, 2, 3

Question 2: A = boiling, spinning and reeling, B = boiling, wringing and treating, C = winding and weaving, D = measuring and making into rolls, E = beating and 'hackling'. The order in which the processes were carried out is as in the caption box.

Back home again

Q1–5: AT1c level 4
Q6: AT1c level 4, AT3 levels 3, 4, 6
Q7: AT1a levels 3, 4
Q8 and Activity: AT1c levels 4, 5, 6, 7, 8

Question 1: Use **Worksheet 23**, as mentioned earlier, to name the places visited by Defoe.

Timeline: The Making of the UK

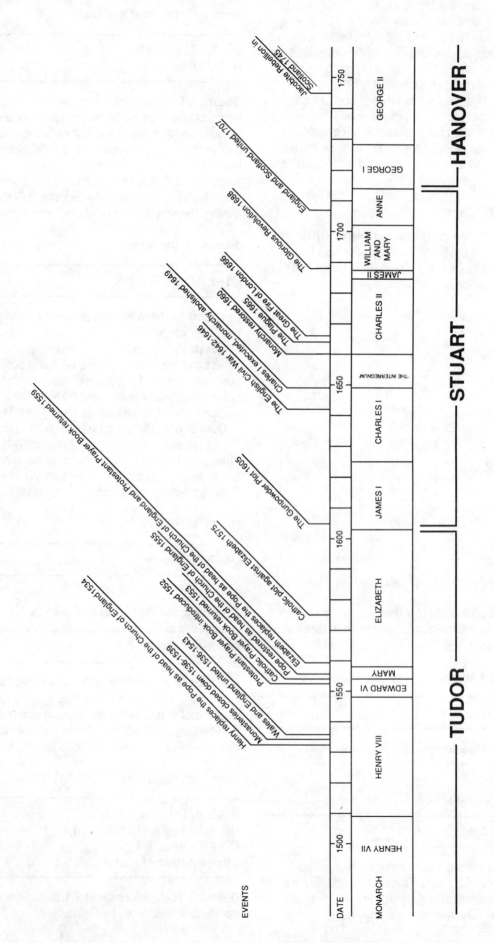

SOCIETIES IN CHANGE THE MAKING OF THE UK

Nicholas Jennings

BEFORE you make your poster, read through Source 2, which was written by Thomas Harman, a Justice of the Peace. It comes from a book he wrote warning people about beggars who were pretending to be poor.

Thomas Harman was in London to visit a printer. From the window of the inn where he was staying Harman saw a beggar outside in the street. He was dirty and covered with blood, but Harman thought he might be a Counterfeit Crank. So with the help of his printer friend he did a bit of detective work.

SOURCE 1 Two of the disguises of Nicholas Jennings

SOURCE 2 From Harman's book

66 *I asked the man where he was born, what his name was, how long he had had this disease, and how long he had been in London and where.*

'Sir,' said he, 'I was born at Leicester. My name is Nicholas Jennings, and I have had this falling sickness eight years. I have been these two years in London, and a year and a half in Bethlehem [a hospital for the insane].'

'What is the name of the keeper of that house?' said I.

'His name is John Smith,' he answered.

'Then,' said I, 'he must know you.'

'Not only he, but the whole house beside,' said this crank.

I went to my room and commanded my servant to go to Bethlehem, and bring me word from the keeper whether any such man had been with him. My servant, returning to my lodging, did say that there was never any such man there.

Then I sent for the printer, told him of the crank, and asked that I might have some servant of his to watch him faithfully that day.

He sent two boys, who did as they were asked, and found the crank about St Paul's. When it began to be dark, the crank went to the waterside, and took a boat and was set over the water into St George's field. One of the boys took a boat and followed him, and the other went back to tell his master.

Soon, the master had taken a boat and crossed over. Now they still had sight of the crank, who crossed over the fields into Newington. The printer stopped him and called for the constable. The constable would have laid him all night in the cage that stood in the street. 'Nay,' said the printer, 'I pray you have him into your house. For this is like to be a cold night and he has few clothes.'

The constable agreed. They had him in and made him wash, and stripped him stark naked.

Then the printer and the constable decided to search a barn for some rogues, a quarter of a mile from the house, and went about their business. The crank, spying all gone, asked the good wife that he might go out to the back of the house to make water. She bade him draw the latch of the door and go out, not thinking he would have gone away naked. But naked as ever he was born, he ran away. 99

Edward Hext

Before you write your report read through this real letter that Edward Hext, Justice of the Peace in Somerset, wrote to the government on 25 September 1596. Don't copy the letter, just use it for ideas.

What does Hext say about:
- why there are so many poor people
- what problems poor people cause
- what to do about the problem of poor people?

SOURCE 1   Letter from Edward Hext, Justice of the Peace in Somerset, to Lord Burghley, concerning the increase of vagrants, 25 September 1596

" *Right honourable and my very good Lord,*

The crimes committed in this county increase all the time. Knowing how much you care about the preserving of peace in this land I give you details of the prisoners this year in Somerset: 183 were arrested. Very few of these came to any good. They nearly all refuse to work. Their limbs are stiff through idleness and they would rather risk being executed than work. I know this to be true because when I sent wandering suspicious persons to the House of Correction they begged me to send them to prison instead because they would be forced to work in the House of Correction.

My good lord, these are not all the thieves and robbers wandering the county. I know that there are many others who are never punished. Many peasants who have their goods stolen refuse to appear in court as witnesses. They say they will not cause men to be executed simply for stealing. Other criminals are allowed to escape by constables who are incapable of doing their job properly.

I do not know how the local people survive. Some of them have been driven to crime by starvation. This year a group of 80 of them stole a whole cartload of cheese.

The large numbers of idle wandering criminals are the main cause of the poverty in this county. They don't do any work and yet spend their time in alehouses eating and drinking excessively. One thief confessed to me that he and others had stayed in an alehouse for three weeks in which time they ate twenty fat sheep and oxen which they stole from the poor local farmers. When these criminals are sent to prison the people who have been robbed by them then have to pay to feed them.

The most dangerous are the wandering unemployed soldiers. There are three or four hundred of these in Somerset. They go about in twos or threes but do all meet up in an alehouse once a week. They are dangerous because they are not afraid of the JPs. At a recent court a sturdy vagrant was ordered to be whipped. He swore a great oath that if he was whipped it would be the dearest whipping for the JPs. They were so afraid of him that he was let off without a whipping.

Your good Lordships in all humbleness to be commanded

Edward Hext "

Was this a good time to be living in England?

Decide who in the group is going to look at which subject.

One statement has already been written for you in each box. Look up the page references and source references shown in your box and then write another two statements in the box.

Make sure you can support your statements from the evidence.

Was this a good time to be living in England?

Wives
Wives didn't own anything — everything they had belonged to their husband

- Sources 12 and 13 on pages 18 and 19

- Right-hand column on page 19

Rich people
Most rich people lived in big, well furnished houses

- paragraphs 2, 3 and 4 on page 3

- Left-hand column on page 14

Husbands
Husbands were allowed to beat their wives

- Source 6 on page 17

- Sources 12 and 13 on pages 18 and 19

Poor people
The number of poor people was increasing

- Source 8 on page 5

- Sources 1 and 2 on page 6

Children
One fifth of all babies died before they were one year old

- Source 8 on page 17

- Source 22 on page 21

Melford Church in the 1520s

Mark on the plan in Source 1 the items mentioned in Source 2.

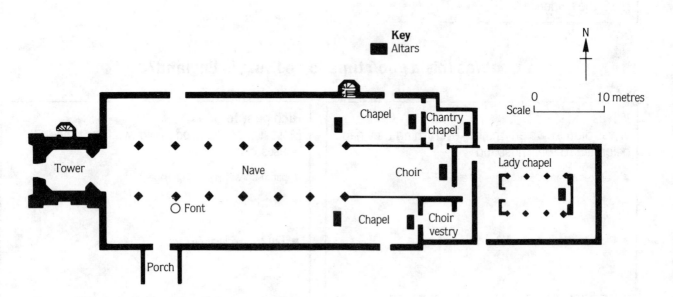

Key
■ Altars

N

0   10 metres
Scale

Tower

Nave

○ Font

Porch

Chapel

Choir

Chapel

Chantry chapel

Choir vestry

Lady chapel

SOURCE 1 Plan of Melford Church

SOURCE 2 A description by Roger Martin of what Melford Church looked like in the 1520s

❝*At the back of the high altar a carving of Christ's crucifixion.*

At the north end of the same altar a large gilt image of the Holy Trinity.

In my chapel at the back of the altar a table with a crucifix on it, with the two thieves hanging.

To the north of the altar from the ground to the roof a painting of Jesus, and to the south a painting of the Blessed Lady.

A rood-loft, with the rood [a crucifix] and Mary and John. The loft going right across the church. On its side, painted, the twelve disciples.

All the roof beautified with gilt stars.

In the vestry many rich copes and vestments.

In the choir, in a recess in the north wall, the sepulchre [the 'tomb' where the leftover bread and wine from Mass were brought].❞

WORKSHEET 6

Portrait of Elizabeth

How to make your portrait of Elizabeth:
Prick through each dot with a pin onto a blank
sheet of paper. Then join up the dots to get the
outline of the Queen's face, hair and shoulders.

Colour or paint the image to make Elizabeth
look as young and beautiful as possible.

N.B. The approved colour scheme for her
clothes is black and white with gold or silver
decoration. At the moment the Queen does not
like red, orange, blue, pink, green or purple
clothes.

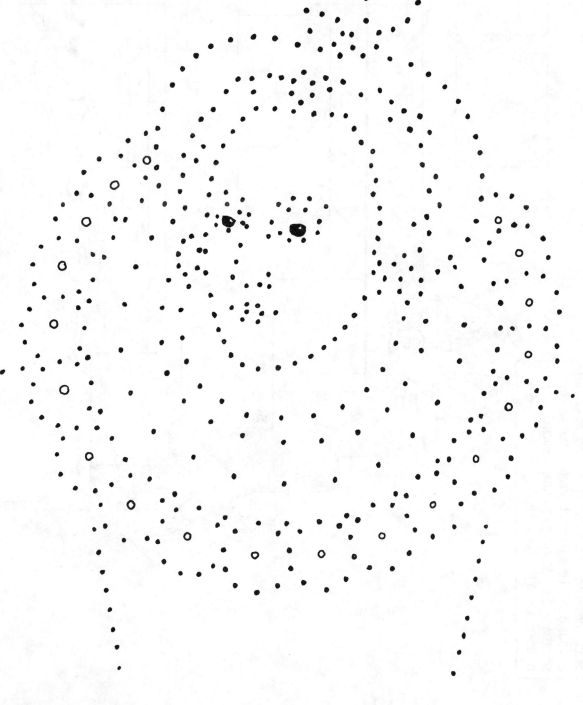

Why did civil war break out in 1642?

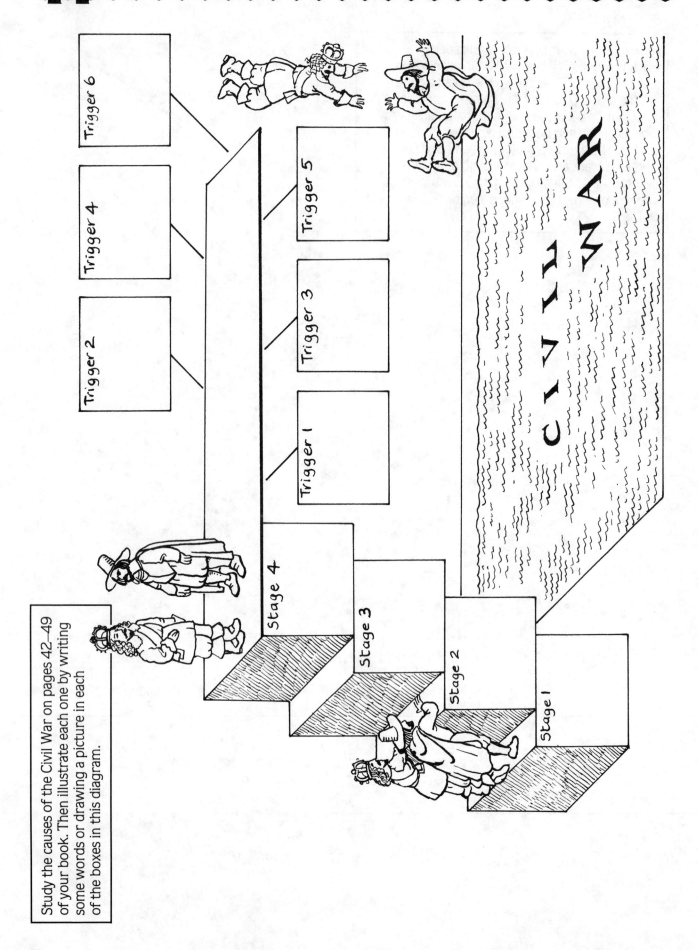

Study the causes of the Civil War on pages 42–49 of your book. Then illustrate each one by writing some words or drawing a picture in each of the boxes in this diagram.

Trigger 6

Trigger 4

Trigger 2

Trigger 5

Trigger 3

Trigger 1

Stage 4

Stage 3

Stage 2

Stage 1

CIVIL WAR

SOCIETIES IN CHANGE THE MAKING OF THE UK

Royalists v. Parliamentarians

Label the following features on these two pictures. You will have to decide which of the two pictures each one applies to. The pictures are on page 51 of your book.

- Leather coat (stained with yellow)
- Iron back and breastplate
- Calibre belt supporting a gun
- Shoulder belt supporting a sword
- Right arm protected by an iron gauntlet
- Head protected by a 'pot' helmet
- Stand to support the musket when firing
- Charges of gunpowder
- Bullets in a round bag

Lady Harley under siege

◆◆◆◆◆◆◆◆◆◆◆◆◆◆◆◆◆◆◆◆◆◆◆◆◆◆◆◆◆◆◆

You are a Royalist soldier besieging Brampton Castle. You have captured one of Lady Harley's servants and found he is carrying these two letters. Can you work out what they mean?

Your teacher can help you.

I desire you imagine to would pray all strength and your father all go together; why did I wrong my judgement so as to to send me let us the word what world . As for to where I did know he would have all be it me do; if I put it is strange away the there was no hold men I shall thirst if be plundered once of it and if I is have no forsaken rents I know I wished that when there not what had been course to for to have seen take in season. If I leave but Brampton there is no art all will be of that ruined.

They say so when all that they gave gloves of gave half a piece to comfort them all for all the losses so they went away crown to every house the soldier to joy of one's heart and the grief of friends what look for enemies out fish they have taken good store. More's lad not been a good horse and he is where is in prison at that loves tobacco Hereford to because never thought it had he was with been so hard a matter hog and dish me. If I had hard of the money to buy come tomorrow I had corn at another and meal else and malt I should not I should hope to render it hold out bravely.

The code breaker

Teacher:
Use a scalpel or sharp Stanley knife to cut out the grey shapes on this worksheet. Be precise. This will create a template for pupils to break the code in the two letters on Worksheet 9.

The Battle of Marston Moor

Use these two plans to show:
- the situation in the middle of the battle
- the situation at the end of the battle

Use the same colour coding as in Source 2 on page 56 of your book, and colour in the key as well.

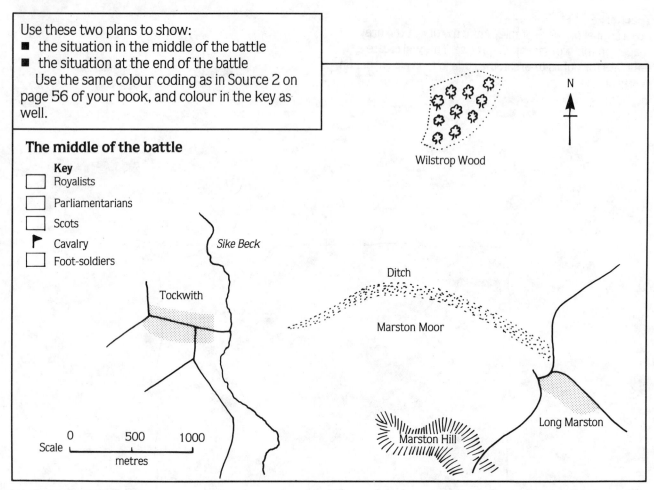

The middle of the battle

Key
- ☐ Royalists
- ☐ Parliamentarians
- ☐ Scots
- ► Cavalry
- ☐ Foot-soldiers

Wilstrop Wood

N

Sike Beck

Ditch

Tockwith

Marston Moor

Long Marston

Marston Hill

Scale
0   500   1000
metres

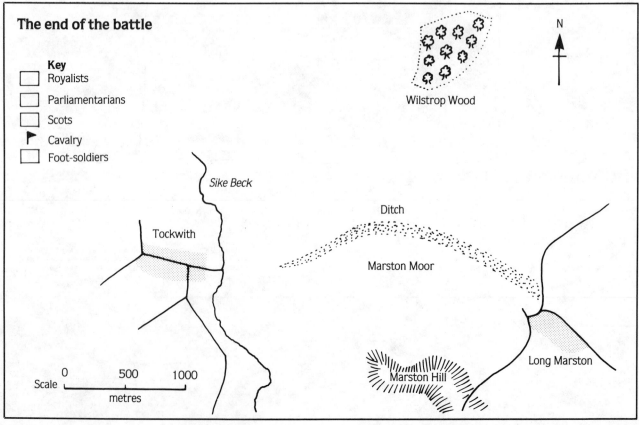

The end of the battle

Key
- ☐ Royalists
- ☐ Parliamentarians
- ☐ Scots
- ► Cavalry
- ☐ Foot-soldiers

Wilstrop Wood

N

Sike Beck

Ditch

Tockwith

Marston Moor

Long Marston

Marston Hill

Scale
0   500   1000
metres

The Civil War in 1645

THE table shows the record made by the Parliamentary commander Thomas Fairfax of what his army did from 15 April to 20 October 1645. Thomas Fairfax was one of the most successful Parliamentary leaders.

We can see from this table the kind of fighting that went on in the Civil War.

1. In what counties did the fighting take place?
2. How many sieges or attacks on cities, towns, castles or houses were there?
3. How many open battles were there?
4. How many men were killed altogether?
5. Were more men killed in open battles than in sieges?
6. From the evidence in this chart do you agree that the Civil War was a war of 'sieges and stormings' and not a war of 'great battles'?

A Table of the Motion and Action of the Army under the

Command of His Excellency *Sir Thomas Fairfax*, From *April* 15. 1645. To *August* 19. 1646. Where in exprest what Battles were fought, what places of strength were taken, whether by storm, or Surrender, the number of Slain, or Prisoners, what Ordnance, Arms, and Colours were taken: The name of the Commander in Chief, the day of the Month when, the C O U N T Y where the A C T I O N was done.

The Month, and Day	The Year	Battles Fought, Places Relieved, Taken, and particular engagements	The manner How	Days of the seige & time of fight	Number of slain in fight or seige	Number of prisoners taken	Number of Ordnance taken	Number of Arms	Number of Colours	The Chief Commander of ours in each design	Commander of the Enemies	The County	Horse
April 15	1645	Rout at Islip	By a party of horses	2 hours	60	230		400	11	Lieut. Gen . *Cromwell*	Earl of *Northhampton*	Oxfordshire	500
April 16	1645	Bletchington house	By a party of horses and dragoons	4 hours		150		450	3	Lieut. Gen . *Cromwell*	Col. *Windebanke*	Oxfordshire	72
April 26	1645	near Farringden	By a party of horses	2 hours	10	40		50	3	Col. *Io. Fienes*		Berkshire	150
April 27	1645	Bampton-Bush	By a party of horses	2 hours		230		200		Lieut. Gen . *Cromwell*	Col. Sir *W. Vaughan*	Oxfordshire	60
May 11	1645	Taunton	By part of the Army	54	204	200		260		Col. *Welden*	General *Goring*	Somersetshire	30
May 22	1645	Oxford	By a party of horses		3	200		200	1	Adjutant. *Flemming*	Capt. *Gardener*	Oxfordshire	12
May 24	1645	Godstow house	quitted		2	10		30		General. *Fairfax*		Oxfordshire	6
June 1	1645	Gaunt house	yielded	3	2	82		100		Col. *Rainsborough*		Oxfordshire	
June 14	1645	Naseby Battle	fought in	2 hours	800	4500	651	8000	112	General. *Fairfax*	Prince *Rupert*	Northamptonshire	200
June 18	1645	Leicester town	yielded	3	6		14	2600	8	General. *Fairfax*	Lord *Hastings*	Leicestershire	300
June 27	1645	Highworth garrison	yielded	1 hour	4	70		180	2	General. *Fairfax*	Major *Hen*	Wiltshire	12
July 3	1645	Taunton	By part of the Army	1 week	1200	400		400		General. *Fairfax*	Lord *Goring*	Somersetshire	460
July 8	1645	Ilchester garrison	quit	1				18		General. *Fairfax*	Col. *Phelips*	Somersetshire	
July 9	1645	Ilmore Fight	By a party of horses	2 hours	50	200		300	9	Major Gen. *Massie*	Lord *Goring*	Somersetshire	300
July 10	1645	Taunton	Fought and quit	1	60	1600	2	2500	32	General. *Fairfax*	Lord *Goring*	Somersetshire	1200
July 13	1645	Burrough hill fort	yielded	4	8	151		200		Col. *Okey*		Somersetshire	
July 23	1645	Bridgewater	stormed	11	30	1600	44	3000	9	General. *Fairfax*	Col. *Windham*	Somersetshire	200
July 30	1645	Bath City	yielded	1		140	6	400	2	Col. *Rich*	Sir *Thomas Bridges*	Somersetshire	11
August 4	1645	Sherborne	routed	1 hour	60	400		600	12	Lieut. Gen . *Cromwell*	Sir *Lewis Dives*	Dorsetshire	
August 15	1645	Sherborne Castle	stormed	16	140	340	19	600	2	General. *Fairfax*	Sir *Lewis Dives*	Dorsetshire	30
August 20	1645	Nunny Castle	yielded	2	5			100		Col. *Rainsborough*	Capt. *Turbervile*	Somersetshire	
August 28	1645	Portshotpoint fort	yielded	6	3		6	140	1	Lieut. Col. *Kempson*		Somersetshire	
Septemb. 10	1645	Bristol City	stormed	18	50	200	151	6000	8	General. *Fairfax*	Prince *Rupert*	Somersetshire	20
Septemb 23	1645	Devizes Castle	yielded	7	5		2	400		General. *Fairfax*	Sir *Charles Lloyde*	Wiltshire	
Septemb 24	1645	Woodcock house	yielded	2						Col. *Pickering*	Col. *Bovill*	Wiltshire	
Septemb 25	1645	Berkley Castle	stormed	9	40	90	11	500		Col. *Rainsborough*	Sir *Charles Lucas*	Gloucestershire	
October 8	1645	Winchester Castle	yielded	6	4		7	500		Lieut. Gen . *Cromwell*	Lord *Oagle*	Hantshire	
October 14	1645	Basing house	stormed	6	40	300	11	500		Lieut. Gen . *Cromwell*	Marq. of *Winchester*	Hantshire	80
October 18	1645	Langford house	yielded	1						Lieut. Gen . *Cromwell*	Sir *Barth. Pell*	Wiltshire	
October 20	1645	Tiverton Castle	stormed	6	4	200	4	400	2	General. *Fairfax*	Sir *Gilbert Talbot*	Devonshire	20

Was Charles a good king?

You are going to judge how good a king Charles I was.

Work in pairs. Below you will find a number of problems Charles faced. For each problem there are three possible courses of action for Charles to take.

You probably remember what Charles actually did, but forget that for the time being. Imagine you are advising Charles in the seventeenth century.

For each problem, decide which of the actions would be most sensible (give that action three points) and which least sensible (give that one point). The remaining action gets two points. The first one has been done for you.

1. It is 1625. Charles must marry to get an heir. Should Charles:
a) marry a daughter of a Protestant English landowner *or* `2`
b) marry a princess from a Catholic country *or* `1`
c) marry a princess from a Protestant country? `3`

2. It is 1652. Parliament has refused to give Charles money from customs duties, which is his main source of income. Should Charles:
a) stand up to Parliament and carry on collecting customs duties anyway *or* ☐
b) do everything that Parliament wants so it will give him the duties *or* ☐
c) arrest all the members of Parliament? ☐

3. It is 1634. Charles is running short of money. Should he:
a) go out and find a job with good wages *or* ☐
b) find methods of getting money which mean he doesn't need Parliament any longer *or* ☐
c) call Parliament and ask for some money? ☐

4. It is 1637. The Archbishop of Canterbury is forcing unpopular changes to the English Church on the people. Should Charles:
a) force the change on Scotland as well *or* ☐
b) stop the changes *or* ☐
c) let the Archbishop do what he likes with the Church? ☐

5. It is 1640. Scotland has invaded the north of England. Should Charles:
a) flee to France *or* ☐
b) pay the Scots £850 a day to stop them causing any more trouble *or* ☐
c) agree to the Scots' demands? ☐

6. It is 1641. Parliament has demanded that the King's unpopular minister Strafford should be executed. Should Charles:
a) promote Strafford to a more important job *or* ☐
b) dismiss Parliament *or* ☐
c) agree to execute Strafford to stop Parliament causing trouble? ☐

7. It is 1642. Parliament continues to cause trouble. Should Charles:
a) blow up the Houses of Parliament *or* ☐
b) send soldiers to arrest the ringleaders *or* ☐
c) write a pamphlet criticising Parliament and circulate it to the gentry? ☐

8. It is 1648. Charles has lost the Civil War. He is a prisoner. Should he:
a) pretend to agree to what Parliament wants and secretly plot with the Scots to fight against Parliament again *or* ☐
b) take up an Open University course *or* ☐
c) agree to everything Parliament wants? ☐

Once you have scored each set of actions look back in your book or find out from your teacher what Charles actually did. Then add up his score, according to the points you have given each action.
8–13: You think Charles was an awful king.
14–19: You think Charles made a lot of mistakes but tried his best.
20–24: You think Charles was a brilliant king.
Compare the score you have given Charles with the score that other members of the class have given him. Do you disagree? If you do, then find out why. Have you scored the actions differently?

The trial of Charles I

Teacher:
Copy and cut up these cards and hand them out to 'witnesses' in the class.

Witness for the prosecution: John Thompson

You are an MP who supported Parliament throughout the Civil War.

You believe the war was Charles' fault. You were there when he came to Parliament to arrest five MPs on 4 January 1642.

You saw Charles' complete contempt for Parliament's rights. You saw that he thought he could get his way by violence and force.

You also believe it was Charles who actually started the war. You were in Nottingham on 22 August when Charles' army set up his standard (his army flag), and so declared that his army was going to fight Parliament's army.

You heard Charles call on all loyal Englishmen to join his army and to fight Parliament to restore him to power.

Witness for the defence: Edward Cotswold

You were loyal to the King throughout the war.

You believe that Charles was driven into the Civil War by Parliament's unreasonable demands. You believe Parliament was acting in its own narrow self-interest, not in the best interests of England.

You believe that Parliament had already started the war by taking control of the army on 22 March 1642. You believe that when the King raised his standard (his army flag) in Nottingham he was only doing what he had to do to defend England's best interests.

Witness for the prosecution: Elizabeth Stiles

You were a servant to the King while he was a prisoner at Carisbrooke Castle on the Isle of Wight.

You have served the King loyally, but you have been called as a witness against him because you were caught carrying letters that Charles wrote to Scottish rebels in January 1648, when he had been a prisoner in Carisbrooke Castle for only one month. These letters asked the Scots to raise an army to fight against Parliament and put him back in power.

You are sad to have to betray your King, but your own life is at risk, and you will be treated more mercifully if you tell your story truthfully.

Witness for the defence or for the prosecution: James Morton

You are a merchant from Dorset. During the Civil War you organised a militia to keep both armies' soldiers out of your county. Your trade depended on keeping Dorset peaceful.

You believe that the Civil War was a battle between King and Parliament alone. It did not concern the majority of people in England.

You believe King and Parliament should patch up their grievances.

If Parliament accepts Charles back as king and works with him England will be more peaceful. England needs a king and a Parliament.

Witness for the defence: Charles Lewis

You are a Royalist army officer who fought in the major battles of the Civil War.

You say that Parliament's army committed atrocities. For example, after Parliament's victory at Montrose all the surviving prisoners were executed as traitors.

In Charles' defence you are able to point out that Charles had a reputation for kindness and generosity, before and during the war. And he did not himself order his officers to commit atrocities.

Witness for the defence: Arthur Walden

You are a clergyman from Yorkshire who supported Archbishop Laud's reforms before the Civil War.

You don't believe that Parliament has any right to sit as a court to judge Charles. You say that only God can judge a king, because only God can choose a king.

You believe that Parliament ought to abandon this trial. Trying the King in this way will produce terrible results in England. No one will believe in the authority of God or of the Church any more.

Witness for the prosecution: Thomas Carter

You are a soldier who changed sides during the Civil War from Royalist to Parliamentarian.

You believe Charles' army was guilty of awful crimes. The soldiers burned towns and villages and attacked and murdered innocent people.

They also tortured prisoners. You say you heard Charles order one of your officers who was mistreating prisoners: 'I do not care if they cut them three times more, for they are my enemies'.

King of England

Application form
Post: King of England

Name:

Age:

Nationality:

Religion:

Married?

Name of wife:

Religion of wife:

Any children:

Use this space to explain why you would be good at this job (for example, describe your past experience, or your personal interests)

Use this space to declare anything that might make you unsuitable for the job

Signed

Date

The English Recorder

Causes and consequences of the English Revolution

Look at these eight cartoons. Some of them show *causes* of the English Revolution and some show *consequences*. Cut them up and stick them into two pages in your book, one for causes and one for consequences.

Then write a sentence under each picture explaining what it shows.

The disunited kingdom

◆◆◆◆◆◆◆◆◆◆◆◆◆◆◆◆◆◆◆◆◆◆◆◆◆◆◆◆◆◆◆◆◆◆

At the end of the arrows on this map write notes and/or draw pictures to show the factors that were making England, Ireland, Scotland and Wales disunited.

The first one has been done for you. You will need to look at page 72 of your book.

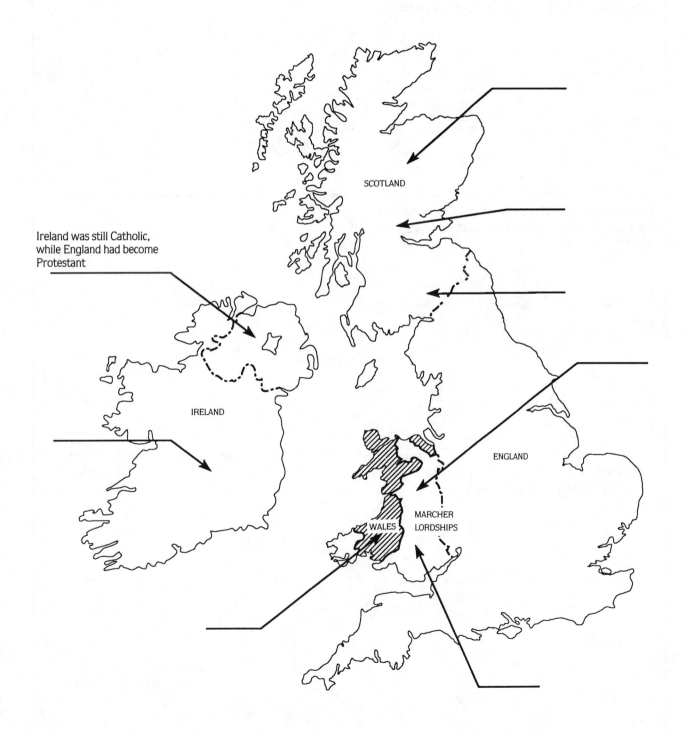

Ireland was still Catholic, while England had become Protestant

SCOTLAND

IRELAND

ENGLAND

MARCHER
LORDSHIPS

WALES

Bonnie Prince Charlie – this is your life!

◆◆◆◆◆◆◆◆◆◆◆◆◆◆◆◆◆◆◆◆◆◆◆◆◆◆◆◆◆

This is your Life:

Running order

Subject:

Introduction: (for example, three or four lines
about why he is famous: his main achievements)

To be interviewed: (show who you will interview,
e.g. friends, colleagues, family, and what you want to
ask them about)

1.

2.

3.

4.

5.

Conclusion: (for example, three or four lines
summing up why people like him)

London grows

◆ ◆ ◆ ◆ ◆ ◆ ◆ ◆ ◆ ◆ ◆ ◆ ◆ ◆ ◆ ◆ ◆

A. This plan shows how London grew from the Middle Ages to 1750. Colour it and then colour the key to show the growth of London.

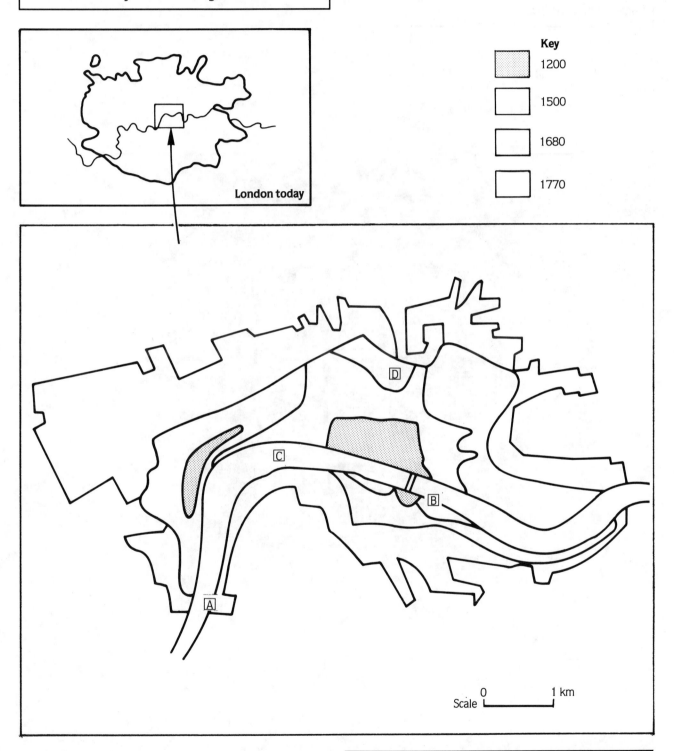

London today

Key

1200

1500

1680

1770

0   1 km
Scale ⊢———————⊣

B. The letters A, B, C and D show four possible positions for the artist of Source 11 on page 85 of your book. Choose the correct one and explain your choice.

A London merchant's house

Put notes around the outside of this drawing to show all the features of this merchant's house.
  You will need to refer to the painting on page 82 of your book.

The Plague

Write notes around the outside of each picture explaining what is going on.

You will need to refer to pages 83 and 84 of your book.

Britain in 1750

Work in groups. You are going to make a wall display showing what life in Britain was like in 1750.

The big map shows all the places visited by Defoe described on pages 88–93 of your book.

1. Label each place correctly. You will need to look at an atlas.
2. Divide the places up between you. Make a drawing and/or write a few sentences about what happened in your place in 1750. Use a separate sheet of paper for each place.
3. When you have finished all your descriptions get a large sheet of paper from your teacher. Cut out the map and stick it in the middle of the sheet. Draw lines from each place to a spot outside the map and then arrange your drawings in their correct places. Your final sheet should look something like this.

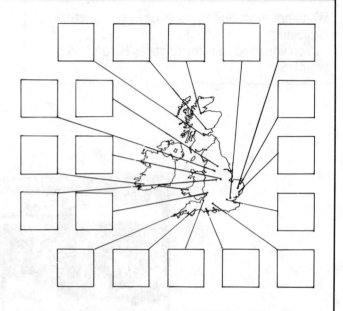

THE FRENCH REVOLUTION

Introduction

In National Curriculum terminology **The French Revolution** is a Category B supplementary study unit involving the study of an episode or turning point in European History before 1914.

It begins by looking at what France was like before the Revolution. It then focuses on the turbulent events of the years 1789–94. Through a range of enquiries it tells the story of the Revolution as it moved from idealism into war and bloodshed. Finally, it investigates selected aspects of Napoleon's rule in France and Europe and sees how far the ideals of the Revolution were continued.

There are many reasons to select this Category B unit.
■ Thematically it links well with the British core unit for Y8, **The Making of the UK**. The monarchies and the revolutions of the two societies are comparable.
■ It covers one of the most significant turning points in European History, including developments and ideas which have influenced events in France and around the world ever since.
■ In our era of European co-operation in some areas and conflict in others it is helpful to study an earlier period of History with similar characteristics. France's attempts to export its Revolution, other neighbouring countries' attempts to stifle change in France, Napoleon's attempt to run Europe as a single entity, the growth of nationalism – all have relevance to recent events in Western and Eastern Europe. They provide a good foundation for the study of twentieth-century European History required in Y9 and in Key Stage 4.
■ The French Revolution raises basic questions about government, democracy, equality and the rights of citizens. It can therefore contribute significantly to the cross-curricular theme of education for citizenship.

In this unit, as with many of the supplementary study units, your pupils have the opportunity to study a subject in depth – something which is just not possible in the core units. Furthermore, as there is no prescribed content for the supplementary study units you also can pick and choose from the enquiries, as long as the broad requirements for Category B units and the full range of ATs are covered. It would be possible, for instance, to omit some of the material on Napoleon and focus on the story of the French Revolution up to 1794. That would still offer a more than adequate coverage of the ATs.

Finally, as with all other units in the series, there is provision in some enquiries for the class to split into study groups. For more guidance about this see page 6 of this book.

THE ATTAINMENT TARGETS

The unit gives an excellent opportunity for working with the full range of Attainment Targets.
■ Essentially, the unit is about change (AT1 strand a). Pupils will be able to see how France was changing before the Revolution and how pressures for more radical change built up. They will study how rapid and violent change can bring about its own problems, and how some people resist change. They will also see how Napoleon set himself to undo what he said were the mistaken changes of the Revolution, while preserving and strengthening the best of them. Pupils will be able to judge for themselves whether he succeeded, or whether he betrayed the Revolution.
■ Causation (AT1 strand b) figures prominently in the unit. Pupils will be able to distinguish between different types of causes of the Revolution (e.g. long-term causes and triggers). They will see how the French Revolution had consequences into the nineteenth and twentieth centuries.

Many of the enquiries focus on a specific aspect of causation: the role of individuals, such as King Louis, Charlotte Corday or Robespierre, and of groups, such as the sans-culottes.
■ The early enquiries in the unit focus on AT1 strand c as we try to reconstruct aspects of life in pre-Revolutionary France. Were all peasants poor? Were all nobles rich? Was the king really all-powerful? Were all members of the Third Estate farmers?
■ The French Revolution has been the subject of intense debate over two centuries – a wide variety of interpretations by successive historians and different societies have illustrated how much a person's viewpoint on the Revolution can be influenced by their circumstances. It is therefore fruitful ground for work towards AT2.

Other aspects of AT2 are also addressed. The process by which Napoleon was rehabilitated from deposed tyrant to fallen hero is investigated. Popular images of the Revolution are also subjected to scrutiny. Was it mainly aristocrats who were guillotined? Was the Bastille really so significant a place that its storming should be commemorated to the present day?
■ Evidence-based enquiry is the mainstay of the unit. Pupils will be confronted by a large amount of evidence from the period and they should acquire the skills to interrogate a wide range of sources (AT3). They will also develop the skills necessary for spotting bias in political cartoons and propaganda, as well as seeing the problems involved in reaching definitive or objective views of History even when a large amount of evidence is available.

FURTHER READING

Teachers may find the following books useful for extending their knowledge of the French Revolution and the Napoleonic Era:

Days of the French Revolution by Christopher Hibbert (Penguin, 1989) (lively)
The Oxford History of the French Revolution by W. Doyle (Oxford, 1989) (more academic)
Citizens by Simon Schama (Penguin, 1989) (a new angle)
Napoleon by V. Cronin (Pelican, 1973) (favourable)
Bonaparte by Corelli Barnett (Allen and Unwin, 1978).

Detailed notes

Section 1: Introduction

ENQUIRY: HOW HAS THE FRENCH REVOLUTION BEEN REMEMBERED?

Pupils' Book pp. 96–99
Worksheets 25, 26

This is a two-spread enquiry. It gets the unit off to a lively start by focusing on two of the most enduring and powerful images of the French Revolution – the guillotine and the storming of the Bastille.

However, pupils are invited to see from the start how the popular images of these events are themselves 'interpretations'. There is therefore scope to develop understanding of both AT2 and AT3 through this enquiry.

To set up this enquiry – indeed the whole unit – it would be helpful to display a range of images of the bicentenary celebrations around the room. Source 1 is only one example.

(Pages 96–97)

The guillotine

Q1: AT3 levels 1, 2, 3

Normally the guillotine is a focal point for popular disgust at the violence of the Revolution. It is associated with the worst excesses of the Revolution. And yet to start with the guillotine represented modernity. It was a move away from the old way of doing things. It was progressive, enlightened, the appliance of science to the problem of delivering a painless death to those who had to die. The old brutality of capital punishment was replaced by a new super efficiency. And the old divisions between punishments for the rich and the poor had been replaced by a more democratic method of execution. The guillotine was a metaphor for the Revolution itself.

Citizenship: There is scope for discussing the rights and wrongs of the death penalty and modern methods for its implementation.

Pupils might like to know that two forerunners of the guillotine existed in Britain. One, the 'maiden', was a massive oak construction with a reinforced blade which was used in Scotland from 1565 to 1710 and which removed some 120 heads. Another is still standing in Gibbet Street, Halifax. Anyone stealing a piece of cloth worth more than thirteen pennies could be beheaded. Fifty culprits were executed by 1650 when its use was discontinued.

One of the many interesting guillotine stories that survive from the Revolution concerns a debate about when exactly a guillotined person died. The story goes that an inquisitive doctor made an arrangement with a condemned man that he would speak to him after his head had been severed. If the doctor's words were understood, the beheaded man would wink. The

experiment was not a success!

N.B. you can find guillotine statistics – numbers killed and class of casualties, etc – on pages 134–135 of the pupils' book.

Questions 1 and 2 are for class discussion.

Question 1: It is very important that pupils realise that Source 2 comes from the time of the Revolution. The image of the guillotine as an instrument of Terror – despite its noble minded start – did not take long to develop. The cartoon cost the artist his life.

Ask pupils if they think Source 2 is literally true. Even so, can it suggest something true about one period of the Revolution (AT3 level 9)?

Question 2 is simply intended to help pupils appreciate the human angle on the guillotine.

You can pull the discussion together by writing the following two statements on the board and asking pupils to say which they most agree with and why.

■ 'The guillotine was a cruel way to execute people and should never have been used.'

■ 'The guillotine has a terrible reputation only because it was used so much.'

N.B. The use of the guillotine continued in France until capital punishment was abolished in 1982. Ten years later, there is a strong popular feeling that it should be brought back for child murderers.

The Bastille

Q1: AT3 level 1
Q2: AT1b levels 2, 3
Q3–4: AT3 levels 2, 3, 4

Revolutions need symbols of tyranny against which to act. The Bastille was used in this way. It represented all that was hateful about the old order in France even if its real function was less spectacular.

The Bastille had been built in the thirteenth century to defend the eastern side of Paris. It had been a most formidable fortress in its time – 80 feet high, with walls fifteen feet thick, and with a wide moat that could be filled from the Seine.

By the eighteenth century, however, Paris had expanded so much that the Bastille had lost its strategic significance and had been taken over as a royal prison – a prison where prisoners were held on *lettres de cachet*, i.e. on the king's or a noble's orders, without trial.

By 1789 the Bastille was no longer needed and plans had already been drawn up for its demolition. Despite its garrison of more than 100 men, it held only seven prisoners. On the face of it, given these facts, Charles James Fox's description of the storming of the Bastille as 'the greatest event that ever happened in the world' seems an unlikely one.

Question 2: Compare it with the dismantling of the Berlin Wall in 1989 and the toppling of Lenin's statues in Eastern Europe. It is an important symbolic act to destroy symbols of oppression.

❀❀❀❀❀❀❀❀❀❀❀❀❀❀❀❀❀❀❀❀❀❀❀❀❀❀❀❀❀❀❀❀❀❀❀❀❀❀❀

Question 3: Remind pupils to look at all the sources on the spread.

(Pages 98–99)

The storming of the Bastille

Q1–2: AT3 levels 1, 2, 3
Q3: AT2 levels 2, 6 and AT3 levels 4, 7
Q4: AT3 levels 1, 2, 3
Q5: AT2 levels 5, 8

There is controversy over the word 'nothing' in King Louis' hunting diary. Some historians use it to show how out of touch he was. Others say we shouldn't read too much into this – it was only his *hunting* diary after all.

In a later conversation with his adviser Rochefoucauld, Louis is reputed to have asked when told about the storming of the Bastille, 'Is it a revolt?' The answer: 'No, it is a revolution.'

You can use **Worksheet 25** – a map of Paris – to help with analysing the events described on this spread, and in later enquiries. Pupils can fill in the boxes with details about the various labelled places as they come across them during the unit.

Question 1: Emphasise that Source 8 is painted by a participant in the events shown. Fruitful discussion can follow on whether his being a participant makes the painting more reliable than versions painted by non-participants.

Worksheet 26 is an outline of Source 8 to be used for question 1.

Question 1 can be tackled in pairs. Ask pupils to show on their outline anything else taking place in the picture. All the key moments in the storming are illustrated.

Sources 13 and 14 introduce the British reaction, which will be returned to a number of times during the unit. At this stage, however, a class discussion on how pupils would expect England to feel about change and revolution across the Channel in France, based on their study of The Making of the UK, could be worthwhile. Have a class vote: who would expect Britain to welcome it, who to oppose it?

Question 5: At this stage pupils have a limited amount of evidence for answering this question. They can point to the significance of the Bastille itself. But they are also being invited to form their own hypotheses about the significance of this event in the Revolution as a whole which they can return to later in the unit.

The attack on the Bastille cost 83 attackers' lives, yet only eight defenders'. The 954 attackers received certificates (as in Source 5) as conquerors of the Bastille. The Assembly ordered the Bastille to be dismantled. Many of the stones were used to make models such as Source 6 on page 97. The Revolution had found its symbol.

Napoleon made a plan at the height of his success to build an enormous bronze elephant on the site. Economic problems caused the plan to be moderated, and a plaster elephant was erected instead, in 1814, which gradually crumbled until it was demolished in 1846.

This book was written in the weeks preceding and following the attempted military coup against President Gorbachev of the former USSR. We were struck by the similarities with the events of the Revolution: for example, a crucial moment being reached when the soldiers of the government refused to fire upon their countrymen.

N.B. There is a timeline on the title page of this unit (pages 94–95) which can be used at regular intervals to orientate pupils. A copy of it to hand out can be found on **Worksheet 24**.

Section 2: Causes of the French Revolution

In his epic work *Citizens*, Simon Schama has a chapter title 'How old was the Old Régime?'. That question underlies all the work in Section 2. A traditional view of the Ancien Régime is of an outdated and doomed government and society. The more complex view, argued by Cobban and Schama, is that change was taking place already in this society, that the relationships and position of the estates were more fluid than might be imagined, and indeed that the Revolution was actually hastened because French society was already changing anyway.

However, the political structure of France had remained largely unchanged for centuries. There were no political changes to reflect the changes in the social structure. This brought untold pressure to bear on the established system.

ENQUIRY: WAS FRANCE WELL GOVERNED BEFORE THE REVOLUTION?

Pupils' Book pp. 100–103

We begin with the traditional view – an outmoded monarchy running a chaotic and inefficient government. And, specifically, the most tangible anomaly of the old régime: an absolute monarch.

The most helpful starting point for pupils may be a comparison with the monarchy in England before the Civil War. They will have some mental picture of the power of the king from their work on The Making of the UK – looking back at Source 3 on page 71 may help remind them. The English king was powerful. And yet he was not nearly as powerful as the French king was 200 years later.

Pupils need to understand the power of the absolute monarch and understand the strengths and weaknesses of the individual in post. They will discover that there was some incongruity between people's perceptions of Louis' suitability and the requirements of the position (AT1c level 6).

N.B. Draw pupils' attention to the glossary on page 170 of the pupils' book. Glossary words are printed in small capitals.

(Pages 100–101)

Q1: AT1c levels 4, 5
Q2: AT3 levels 1, 3, 4
Q3–4: AT3 levels 3, 4
Q5: AT1b level 2
Q6: AT1b level 6
Q7: AT2 level 5

The king

The implications of Sources 1 and 2 should be discussed thoroughly in class so that good answers can be generated for **question 1**.

Louis XVI

To strengthen pupils' feel for the type of person Louis was, and to help prepare them to answer questions 2 and 3, the class can do the following character mime.

Split into groups of three. Read Source 4. You have five minutes to prepare a silent mime which shows Louis' strengths and weaknesses.

A similar mime can be devised for Marie Antoinette.

Marie Antoinette

Parallels can be drawn with the furore caused by Charles I's marriage to Henrietta Maria (page 42). Intermarriage between the royal families of Europe was the norm. It was a way of strengthening alliances.

Question 7 raises a recurring theme in history and in everyday life today. For example, schools abound in rumour – innocent and malicious – which no amount of evidence seems to be able to shift. Pupils may have heard things said by others – even about themselves – which they know to be patently untrue. Yet they are believed: 'No smoke without fire,' people might say.

As far as the study of history goes, pupils need to realise that both aspects of question 7 are important. We do need to evaluate whether these things were true. But for questions of causation, as in this section of the book, what people believed to be true is actually more important.

You might like to tell pupils the story of the Diamond Necklace Affair, which is recounted at length by Cobban in his *Aspects of the French Revolution*. In explanation he says, 'There is a tendency these days to underestimate the part that the trivial, the apparently irrational, the accidental, plays in history . . .' Yet the trivial, soap opera quality of the Affair of the Diamond Necklace should not disguise the deep impact it had on public opinion of Marie Antoinette and the royal court.

There are three main characters to the story: an ambitious young noblewoman, Jeanne de Valois, an ambitious cardinal, Rohan, who was out of favour with the Queen, and the Queen herself. Add to this an exquisite necklace with 579 purest diamonds, made for the Queen but which she (publicly) had declined to buy because she knew it could not be afforded.

Jeanne de Valois convinced Rohan that she could mend the rift between him and Marie Antoinette. She faked letters from the Queen to Rohan. She even faked a midnight meeting between them in the grounds of the palace at Versailles – dressing up a young servant girl, Nicole, in Marie Antoinette's clothes.

Rohan was convinced that Jeanne de Valois did have the Queen's confidence – although in reality she was not close to the Queen at all. He was ready to do anything to please the Queen. So when Jeanne explained that the Queen wanted Rohan's credit to purchase the necklace he duly obliged.

He bought the necklace, and handed it over to Jeanne to be sent to the Queen.

Needless to say, it never got there – Jeanne, her husband and their accomplices lived grandly for a short while on the proceeds of selling the diamonds.

When the fraud came to light, all of them, including Rohan, were imprisoned in the Bastille. Their nine-month trial was the talking point of France. Jeanne gained star status with energetic lies in her defence. The story had all the elements of scandal that our tabloids would relish today. When Rohan was acquitted he was fêted as a hero. Jeanne, however, was finally sentenced to be whipped, branded on each shoulder and then to serve out a life sentence in prison. She escaped nine months later.

Yet much damage had been done to the Queen. The really significant consequence of the affair – for historians at least – is that the reputation of Marie Antoinette and the royal household had been thoroughly tarnished.

Marie Antoinette's reputation today is probably most famously influenced by her comment on the Versailles bread marchers: 'Let them eat cake.' The remark is often taken to show her arrogance. A contrary view points out that a) there is no hard evidence she ever said this, and b) 'cake' is a mistranslation of the word *brioche*, which was the alternative that bakers sold when bread was in short supply. It might have been a sensible suggestion in that context. Rousseau mentions a similar saying in his *Confessions* (1740), which suggests that it was in common usage.

(Pages 102–103)

The second spread looks at other aspects of government under the Ancien Régime. It allows the pupils to access AT1b levels 1–6.

Their conclusions will be based on source evaluation, AT3 levels 1–6.

Local government

The significance of Sources 7 and 8 is as a contrast with the reorganised departments after the Revolution (see page 118).

✠✠✠✠✠✠✠✠✠✠✠✠✠✠✠✠✠✠✠✠✠✠✠✠✠✠✠✠✠✠✠✠✠✠✠✠✠✠

Law and order

Pupils have already considered the way that the guillotine was an attempt to make the death penalty in France more humane. Sources 9–11 give a further impression of the harshness of punishments before the Revolution.

Q1: AT1c level 6, AT3 levels 3,4
Q2: AT2 level 7

Question 2 invites an interim judgement based on the past three pages. The same idea is returned to in the Activity on page 103.

The estates

Q3: AT3 levels 3, 4
Activity: AT1b levels 3, 4, 5, 6, 7

Source 12 gives the stereotypical traditional view of the Ancien Régime. This will be contrasted with a more realistic view in Source 1 on the next page, so discuss Source 12 carefully. Pupils may need reminding how the Feudal System worked.

The estates system can be modelled physically – much as the Roman Republic was modelled in the classroom in *Contrasts and Connections*. Map out four areas of the classroom to represent the four divisions. One person is the king, a few are the clergy and a few are nobles. The majority are peasants.

Hand out four bags of 'money', with the biggest going to the king and the next biggest to the clergy and nobility, etc. The peasants should only get a small bag to share. Emphasise that in the estates system, the further up the pyramid you were the richer you were.

This model can be returned to and adapted to show the actual situation in eighteenth-century France (see notes on pages 104–105 below).

Activity: Sources 13–14 give some of the more obvious criticisms of this system, which can help prime pupils' work for the activity.

Emphasise that the criticism of the estates system was not limited to those at the bottom of the heap.

The **Activity** works as a summary question to establish an initial view of pre-revolutionary France.

ENQUIRY: WHAT WAS LIFE LIKE BEFORE THE REVOLUTION?

Pupils' Book pp. 104–109
Worksheet 27

This three-spread enquiry will show that the lifestyle of each estate cannot be stereotyped. There were poor nobles and poor clergy. There were starving peasants and there were healthy successful peasants. There were rich middle-class businessmen, a whole new class.

Pupils will begin to evaluate who might lose and who might gain from revolutionary change in France.

(Pages 104–105)

Q1: AT1a levels 3, 4
Q2a): AT1c level 6, AT3 levels 1, 2, 3
Q2b)–c): AT3 levels 1,2, 3
Q2d): AT1b level 2

Question 1: If you modelled the traditional view of the estates system in the classroom, do the same for Source 1 before tackling question 1. It will be the easiest way to fix in pupils' minds the differences between the stereotypical view and the actual picture.

Mark out areas of the classroom to correspond with Source 12 on the previous page. Send people into their respective 'estate' area. Emphasise again that the further up you are the wealthier you are. Distribute 'money' or tokens as before.

Now divide the Third Estate into four groups – the largest still peasants, the next largest the urban workers, the next the landless labourers and finally the smallest section the middle classes.

Then, following the information in Source 1, send the majority of the clergy and the majority of the nobility down the scale.

Cream off the middle-class section of the Third Estate and push them up the scale.

Likewise, cream off a few peasant members of the Third Estate and push them further up the scale.

Redistribute the available wealth according to people's new position in the social system.

Source 1: We have continued the colour coding for each estate that has been used in the diagram into the rest of the enquiry – yellow for clergy, blue for nobility and shades of green for the Third Estate.

The First Estate: the clergy

Q1–2, 4: AT3 levels 1, 3, 7   **Q3:** AT3 levels 3, 7

The clergy were powerful even though not all of them were rich. They had strong connections with the nobility – as Source 4 reminds you. Many clergy came from noble families.

Question 2: point pupils to Source 3, particularly to compare the village priest and the skilled craftsman.

Question 3 accesses the ideas in levels 3 and 7 of AT3. Many of the visuals in this unit are political cartoons. It is worth interrogating some of these in detail at the start of the unit. It would become repetitive to ask constantly about reliability and bias, but if the discipline is learned at this early stage it will become an automatic reaction for pupils to see the political purpose of these cartoons. Unfortunately, it has often been difficult to put a precise date on many of them.

In Source 5 discuss:
■ Who is riding in the cart? What belongings is he taking with him (chamber pot, commode, turkeys, including one cooked on a spit, bedding, dovecote)?

■ Who are all the people with him?
■ Does this cartoon praise or criticise the wealth of the Church?

The original caption reads: 'The clergy move out. "I have lost my living. Nothing equals my sadness."'

(Pages 106–107)

The Second Estate: the nobility

Activities: AT1c levels 4, 5, 6, 7, 8, AT3 levels 1, 3, 4

Not all noble families were rich. And by no means all were dead wood. Many of them were involved in industry and business.

However, they were enormously privileged by both the taxation system and the feudal rights.

Source 10: Pupils might compare the grandeur of the chateaux with the houses of the rich studied in Unit A (page 13).

Activity 1: We deliberately set up the stereotypical view to start with: the nobility as lazy, privileged and uncaring. This accesses levels 4 and 5 of AT1c.

Activity 2: With reference to a further set of sources, the nobility are given the 'right of reply'. This second activity allows pupils to access levels 5–8 in AT1c.

The Third Estate: the middle classes

Q1–2: AT3 levels 1, 2, 3, 4
Q3: AT1c levels 6, 7

The middle classes can be seen as a fairly powerless class (politically), but with political aspirations to match their financial ones.

Question 3 aims to encourage pupils to think about what gives a government the right to govern.

The Third Estate: the urban workers

Q1: AT3 levels 3, 4

Source 18 challenges the view given in the text that all urban workers had a miserable life and worked in squalor. This continues to encourage pupils to avoid the stereotypical view.

(Pages 108–109)

The Third Estate: the peasantry

Q1: AT3 levels 1, 3
Q2, 7: AT3 level 3
Q3: AT3 level 7
Q4: AT2 levels 4, 6
Q5: AT3 level 4
Q6: AT3 levels 3, 4, 7, 8, 9

The peasantry in the main had a difficult life.

Source 20: Note the rabbits. They are eating the peasant's crops, but he is not allowed to kill them because the nobles have exclusive hunting rights.

Question 4: This raises an AT2 issue. Are women and their situation deliberately excluded from history books? And if so, why?

Question 6: The focus is nominally on Arthur Young. Young was an English journalist and farmer. In England he experimented with new agricultural methods and wrote about new farming ideas in his *Annals of Agriculture*. From 1768 he began travelling round Britain studying farming methods and comparing different systems. He then made several extensive tours of France between 1787 and 1790. He recorded his observations in great detail. His contacts ranged widely from nobles to peasants, and he talked to many ordinary people. Although very critical of the evils of pre-revolutionary France, he also later criticised the evils of the Revolution. He admitted editing his diary in 1792 to make it less critical of the Ancien Régime. Despite this, historians have frequently used his writings as evidence of the state of France before the Revolution.

It is interesting to compare some of his observations of conditions in Britain, as in the following description of Hertfordshire, from a report to the government's Board of Agriculture in 1804. The extracts show Young's characteristic concern with the plight of the poor.

> 66 *In the present state of this kingdom, I must consider this object [reporting on the plight of the poor] as the most important enquiry that can come under the attention of a County Surveyor. The county's vicinity to the Metropolis secures higher wages, and more constant employment than in many other districts; women can earn £1 1s a week; and some clever little girls even 15s. Good earnings are a most happy circumstance, which I wish to see universal.* 99

Source 23: There were successful peasant landowners in France. But pupils will not need pointing to the amazement with which Arthur Young greeted this finding. It was hardly commonplace.

Question 7: The existence of famine and the consequent need to distribute bread can condemn the king and his régime. That he was attempting to alleviate famine can be praised. Pupils may be well aware of this same dilemma concerning aid to Third World countries. The existence of famine condemns the rich world even if the attempts to alleviate it are sincere and praiseworthy.

❉❉

The Third Estate: the landless labourers

Source 25: Sebastien Vauban was a French military engineer who after a successful army career became a Marshal of France. In 1707 he wrote his *Dime Royale* in which he documented the faults of the French government and in particular discussed taxation. Many of his recommendations anticipated the reforms of the Revolution. His work was banned by the government.

As a support activity which also allows comparisons to be made with the previous unit, ask pupils to suggest items to go in a time capsule intended to give people in 200 years' time a feel for the real situation of people in France before the Revolution. They should put in one item for each of the estates and say why they have chosen this item.

Q1: AT2 levels 5, 6, 7
Q2: AT1c levels 4, 5

The **summary questions** pull together the main themes on the nature of the Ancien Régime. They attempt to establish an overview of pre-revolutionary France. Pupils should look at all of pages 100–109 for evidence. **Worksheet 27** is for use with question 2.

Pupils should also consider the question 'Was a revolution now inevitable?' – an idea familiar to them from work on the English Civil War. The traditional view of eighteenth-century France was that it was so fixed in its backwardness that the only way it could be reformed was by revolution. Many historians now challenge this view. Simon Schama, for instance, says: 'Had the Revolution not taken place the old social structure would still have crumbled, earlier in one place, later in another, only it would have gone on crumbling a piece at a time, instead of collapsing all at once.'

Pupils will be able to demonstrate understanding across a range of levels in AT1a.

We want pupils to end up with the view that changes were already taking place. The next enquiry examines the acceleration of those changes during the eighteenth century.

ENQUIRY: CHANGES IN FRANCE

Pupils' Book pp. 110–113
Worksheets 28, 29, 30

One way or another France was changing even before the Revolution. But the second half of the eighteenth century saw change accelerating. Problems for the king and government were multiplying, and attempts at reform were failing. The text in this two-spread enquiry describes the main economic, social and intellectual changes taking place during the eighteenth century (AT1 strand a). The questions and the concluding activity analyse how these changes helped to cause the Revolution (AT1 strand b).

(pages 110–111)

Economic and social changes

Q2: AT1a level 3, AT1b level 3
Q3: AT1a levels 3, 4, AT1b levels 3, 4

Economic hardship can lead to demands for change – modern examples abound, for example in the Soviet Union and Eastern Europe. Yet economic success can also lead to demands for change. This may be a difficult idea for pupils to grasp and will need some discussion and explanation.

Questions 1–3 are intended for class discussion rather than written work.

Question 3: explain the difference between a hypothesis and a guess.

Taxation

Q2: AT1b level 3
Q3–6: AT3 levels 3, 4
Activity: AT1b levels 2, 3, 4, 5, 6, AT1c levels 4, 5, 6, 7, 8, 9

Questions 1 and 2: Direct taxation is usually seen as more progressive. This is a good opportunity for fostering pupils' economic awareness.

Source 4 shows the taxation breakdown for France before the Revolution. The equivalent breakdown for the UK in 1991–92 was 55% direct and 45% indirect.

Pupils can discuss how indirect taxes today e.g. VAT are different from direct taxes, e.g. income tax. Is it fair that we have been moving away from direct taxation towards indirect taxation over the past decade?

Question 3: Pupils can practise some basic budgeting – an important part of economic awareness.

Question 6: Do a detailed interrogation of Source 6 in a class discussion.

Activity: Before pupils start their work on this activity, discuss the pros and cons of each option thoroughly. That way pupils will generate better answers and display much deeper awareness. Draw a chart on the board like this and write up the pros and cons on the basis of class discussion:

Proposal	Pros	Cons
Reduce expenditure Raise taxes Tax according to wealth Improve tax collection Borrow more money		

(Pages 112–113)

New ideas

Many of the new ideas stemmed from the Scientific Revolution, which pupils have already studied on pages 78–80. France was as much a centre of these developments in the eighteenth century as England had been in the seventeenth.

One notable example of this was the Encyclopaedia of Diderot, which gathered together social and scientific insights from around Europe and enlisted most of the fiercest critics of the Ancien Régime in writing entries. It showed advances in agriculture, engineering, industry and health, and helped fuel the demands for modernisation.

Question 1: The aim is to appreciate the power of tradition. Pupils will probably have strong ideas on some school and family rules. In this fairly easy way they will be able to see in practice how traditions are made and kept.

The American War of Independence

Q1–2: AT1b level 2, AT1c levels 6, 7
Activity Q1: AT1b levels 2, 3, 4, 5, 6, 7
Activity Q2: AT1b level 2, AT1c levels 6, 7, 8, 9

The **Activity** is a wide-ranging exercise summing up much of the ground covered by the unit so far.

Worksheet 28 provides a version of Source 9 for pupils to fill in themselves. It should be enlarged to A3 size. First of all pupils should use the sources suggested to describe each feature briefly. Then, working as a group or in pairs, they should cut out the characters on their worksheet and decide which feature the characters would be most discontented about. There are many possibles and the discussion that will ensue will be the main learning experience.

Pupils will probably put the peasant by either e, f, or i; the urban worker by f or i; the noble by d or h; and the businessman by a or i. We have included b and c as important causes of the Revolution, but they were not, of course, sources of discontent.

Worksheet 29: Pupils can conclude this activity by writing thoughts or words in a word bubble for each character, expressing their discontent.

Worksheet 30 provides an exercise investigating the similarities and differences between the causes of the English and French Revolutions.

ENQUIRY: WHY DID REVOLUTION ERUPT IN 1789?

Pupils' Book pp. 114–117

In this two-spread enquiry we investigate the events of 1788 and 1789 which finally triggered the Revolution. Pupils have already been introduced to the difference between long-term causes and triggers in the context of the English Revolution, and this will help strengthen their grasp of these concepts in AT1 strand b.

(Pages 114–115)

Trigger 1: Economic slump

Q1: AT1b level 2, AT1c level 7

Trigger 2: Calling the Estates General

Q1: AT3 level 3
Q2: AT1b levels 3, 4
Q3: AT1b level 2

In many ways the decision to call the Estates General was a revolution in itself. It was a tacit admission that the government needed the co-operation of its people to rule effectively. The government was bankrupt. It was unable to raise any more money either by taxes or loans and was losing co-operation from the privileged groups who were vital to the running of the country.

But by calling the Estates General expectations were raised. Nobles hoped to dominate it and control any reforms. The Third Estate expected it to solve their immediate financial problems.

From the start the Estates General got bogged down in procedural arguments and quarrels between the estates. From May peasants throughout France took matters into their own hands, attacking the nobles' houses and burning the documents showing their feudal dues.

Meanwhile, in Paris, the radicals in the Third Estate rejected their traditional status as inferior. They wanted their votes to count equally with those of the other estates. They demanded that all estates should reconvene as equals in a National Assembly.

Louis precipitated a crisis by barring the doors of the Assembly. The delegates went to the nearest large building, a tennis court, and swore their famous oath.

Question 3: The aim was to break with the past and to break down the estates system with its implications of rigid hierarchy.

Revolution

Q1: AT1b level 2, AT1c level 7
Q2: AT1b levels 3, 4, 6, 7, 8

Question 2: Modern examples, e.g. Gorbachev, can be cited.

(Pages 116–117)

Q1: AT1a level 1
Q2: AT1b levels 3, 4
Q3: AT1b level 2
Q4: AT1b levels 2, 4
Summary Q1: AT1b levels 3, 5
Summary Q2, 4: AT1b level 6
Summary Q3: AT1b level 5
Activity: AT1b levels 2, 3, 4, 5, 6, 7, 8, 9, AT1c levels 6, 7, 8

Question 2: Feudalism had been dismantled by the peasants themselves when they burned their feudal documents. The nobles' support for this move can therefore be seen as making a virtue out of a necessity.

Activity: This can open up the highest levels of AT1b. Get pupils to compare their answers carefully to see the wide range of reasons that could have contributed to someone's decision to join the attack.

Section 3: How did the Revolution change France?

Now follow six enquiries which try to give pupils a flavour of the times. The period 1789–94 was one of crisis and turmoil. There were great ideals and yet colossal problems.

We have attempted to personalise the political changes by focusing on Louis and his fate.

We have also looked at the increasing influence of the radicals following the outbreak of war.

Throughout the section pupils will see that change is not once and for all: it is continuous. And it is not uniform: for some people things change, for others they do not.

ENQUIRY: DID THE REVOLUTION MAKE FRANCE A FAIRER COUNTRY?

Pupils' Book pp. 118–121

The Declaration of the Rights of Man

Q1: AT1b levels 3, 6

Source 1: Following the American example France was the first European country to have a written constitution. Most other European countries followed France's example. Nowadays the UK is almost alone in Europe in never having adopted a written constitution.

The pupils will have ample opportunity in these two spreads to think about the nature of government and individual rights. There is great potential for work on citizenship as pupils are introduced to some key terms such as 'constitution' and 'democracy'.

Interrogate **Source 1** in detail. Who is who? What are they doing? The estates have been brought together as one nation, all parts of which are to be involved in determining the type of government.

N.B. The term constitution is explained in the glossary, but may need additional discussion.

Source 2 needs careful discussion to pull out the principles on which the revolutionary government was to be based. Reference is made to these at various stages further on in the text.

When answering **question 1** pupils should be asked to consider one by one the king, the nobles, the clergy, the

middle classes and the peasants. They might have to be reminded of the position of these classes in the Ancien Régime.

Question 2 is a citizenship question that also touches on AT1c level 2. Where do you draw the line on what people can write and say? An example in Britain is our law against incitement to racial hatred.

N.B. Comparisons can be made with the effects of the unshackling of publishing and printing after the English Civil War (page 68).

Putting the Declaration into practice

Q1: AT3 level 3
Q2: AT1b level 2
Q3: AT1b levels 2, 3
Q4: AT1a levels 3, 6
Q5: AT1c level 2
Q6: AT 1c level 4
Q7: AT1a level 3, AT1b level 3

Taken together these questions also access AT1a levels 3, 4 and 5 and even the higher levels 6 and 7 as pupils see how changing ideals into actual practice isn't an easy process.

The sources on this spread cover a range of reforms, which are also continued on the next spread. As they cover a lot of ground you may decide to use them selectively with pupils. However, it is the extensive range of the reforms that is part of the point. Most aspects of society were touched. So try to ensure that all aspects are investigated by at least some groups in the class. This exercise forms essential background to the later enquiry on whether Napoleon betrayed the Revolution (page 150).

We have broken down the reforms into categories so that they can be more easily digested, but in practice there are many areas of overlap between the categories.

Each set of reforms will require thorough discussion. As you take each point you could compare it with:
■ the stated ideals of the Revolution – particularly as expressed in the Declaration of the Rights of Man
■ the situation in Britain today. This has constant application not only to AT1c level 2, but also to citizenship education.

Question 3: The title King of the French emphasised that Louis was king by the consent of the people rather than by divine right. He belonged to the French people, as it were. Point pupils to the fact that he still had power. For example, he still had the power to delay laws (Source 3). They will all too easily slip into the view that the Revolution had stripped him of all power.

Questions 5 and 6: The questions are designed to address both how useful these electoral changes were to France and also how democratic our system in Britain is compared with that of revolutionary France (of the figures in Source 6 only deputies (MPs) and some local officials are elected).

The other side of the coin for question 6 is whether there are any advantages that we are missing by not electing these posts. This can create a lively classroom discussion.

Pupils can discuss whether elections ought to be used for more posts in Britain. Pupils might comment that judges often seem out of touch.

(Pages 120–121)

Q1: AT3 level 3
Q2: AT1a level 3, AT1b level 3
Q3: AT3 level 3
Q4: AT1b levels 3, 4
Q5: AT1c level 3
Q6: AT1b level 3

This spread looks at some positive aspects of changes made by the Revolution in business, law, trade and society. However, it also clearly highlights that not everyone was to benefit to the same extent from the reforms of the Revolution, and takes as case studies slaves and women.

Source 9: Merit and civil marriages may need explaining.

Question 2: The two cartoons are a handy summary of how the Revolution has changed the relationship of the estates . . . in theory at least. (Notice what has now happened to the rabbits.)

Question 3: Pupils might be expected to state, however, that this is the ideal of the Revolution, not what necessarily occurred.

Question 5: Basing tax on ability to pay has been a big issue in Britain since the Poll Tax was introduced and then abolished.

Question 6: Trial by jury may need explanation.

Liberty was not for all

Q1: AT1a levels 3, 4, 5, 6, 7
Q2: AT1b levels 3, 4, AT3 level 3
Q3: AT1a levels 4, 6, 7
Summary Q1: AT1a levels 3, 4, 5, 6, 7, AT2 level 7
Activity: AT1c levels 6, 7

Source 13: Compare it with Source 1 on page 68.

Source 15: The woman is holding a document headed *Le moniteur*. Pupils can be asked to write their own news sheet – the Monitor – which aims to offer a women's perspective, monitoring progress made by the Revolution.

Source 16: People defended their economic self-interest despite their stated ideals.

Summary question 1 allows the pupils to access levels 6 and 7 of AT1 strand a. Discuss beforehand what pupils think the term 'fairer' might mean in this context, e.g. people treated more equally, or more justly?

The following idea can be used to help pupils structure their views:

Less fair						More fair				
5	4	3	2	1	Who chose the government	1	2	3	4	5
5	4	3	2	1	Election of officials	1	2	3	4	5
5	4	3	2	1	Taxes	1	2	3	4	5
5	4	3	2	1	Church wealth	1	2	3	4	5
5	4	3	2	1	Legal system	1	2	3	4	5
5	4	3	2	1	Feudal system	1	2	3	4	5

Pupils should give France a score on each count. They will be able to demonstrate that it all depended on who you were as to whether France was a fairer country.

Activity: This again is designed to provoke opportunities for citizenship education.

ENQUIRY: WHAT SHOULD BE DONE WITH THE KING?

Pupils' Book pp. 122–127
Worksheet 31

The flight to Varennes was a gamble for Louis. Up to that point he had managed a passable pretence of going along with the revolutionary changes – even approving them. Many radicals, however, must have had their suspicions of his real commitment to the Revolution. For many of them the flight to Varennes confirmed these suspicions.

This three-spread enquiry considers the King's position in the Revolution. Was he a supporter or a reluctant co-operator? While studying the interesting story of the flight to Varennes, pupils learn something of the character of Louis and his deficiencies as an organiser.

We also investigate whether the flight was really necessary. Consideration is given to Louis' apparently contradictory views on the way the Revolution was going.

Finally, the influence of the war on Louis' fate and on the Revolution is considered.

Throughout the enquiry pupils will have a chance to think again about what the basis for power in a country should be. Specifically, they will be able to decide whether the King could be accommodated, or even wanted to be accommodated, within the revolutionary changes.

This is primarily approached as a good story. However, the pupils have the opportunity to start considering why the King might have tried to get away, and what the Assembly should do with the troublesome monarch. They will have some chance to judge Louis both as a person and as a king.

✿✿✿

(Pages 122–123)

The plan unfolds

Begin by reading out the newspaper account in class and looking at Source 1, before setting pupils to work on the cartoon strip using questions 1, 2 and 3 as a way in.

Q1–3: AT1b levels 2, 3, 4, 5, 6
Activity: AT1b levels 2, 3, 4, AT1c levels 4, 5, 6, AT3 levels 3, 4

Activity: Worksheet 31 provides a blank for the front page of their newspaper, which should be enlarged to A3 size. This is a good opportunity for IT work, especially for the use of a DTP system.

(Pages 124–125)

Why did the King try to flee?

Q1: AT3 levels 1, 3   **Q3:** AT1b levels 2, 3, 4
Q2: AT3 levels 6, 7, 8, 9   **Q4:** AT1b level 3

Sources 4–10: Pupils could work in groups of six to answer **question 1**, taking one written source each and reporting to the rest of the group. Then as a group they should decide which source is likely to be the nearest to Louis' real attitude. **Question 3** can then be a group decision.

What was to be done with the King?

Activity: AT1b levels 4, 5, 6, 7, AT1c levels 4, 5, 6, 7, 8

Sources 11 and 12 illustrate the pressures on the National Assembly. Pupils must see the international pressures as well, as described at the foot of the Activity.

  Activity: The pupils are attempting to see these options as they would have been seen at the time. How pupils score each option and the reasons they give for their choice will show whether they have understood this situation from the perspective of people at the time. All the options are possibilities.

  An alternative support activity, or an activity to prepare for the main activity, is to ask the pupils to write two pieces entitled 'The King should stay' and 'The King should go'. In each they should use the evidence in these sources to make a case for the appropriate point of view.

  In this way pupils can develop some views on what Louis has done right and wrong.

(pages 126–127)

Should France go to war?

Q1: AT3 levels 1, 2, 3
Q2: AT1b levels 2, 3, 4, AT3 levels 2, 3
Q3: AT1b level 2, AT3 levels 3, 4
Q4: AT1b levels 3, 4, 5

The declaration of war was a turning point for France, for the Revolution and, most immediately, for Louis. On this spread we investigate how the outbreak of war, desired by most factions in France, brought about, indirectly, the execution of the King and then the Terror.

  Sources 14–18: There are other reasons which could be added, e.g. some politicians hoped that war would force opponents of the Revolution to declare their hands; some businessmen believed that war would stimulate the economy and they would get a big profit by supplying the army.

  Question 3c) considers the general issues raised by the start of a war. When is it justified? Why are voices of opposition (in this case Robespierre) usually lone voices?

The war goes badly

It would be interesting here to do a predictive exercise. Put away the pupils' book (Source 19 would be too much of a distraction) and explain to pupils that the war is now going very badly. Pupils should each write one thing which they think is likely to happen now to ordinary people, to Louis, to the economy, etc. They should write it on a piece of card and these should be put in a sealed envelope to be opened at the next lesson, when the actual results will be investigated.

The storming of the Tuileries

If you blink you might miss it! The overthrow of the King and the proclamation of a Republic is a crucial event and pupils need to have their attention drawn to it.

The September massacres

Q1: AT1b levels 2, 3, 4, 5
Q2: AT1a level 3, AT1b level 3, AT1c levels 5, 6

At this point in the story pupils can consider whether the Revolution is becoming more violent. At the Bastille only one defender was killed during the fighting, but about seven were killed after its capture. The attackers lost 83.

  Compare this with the interesting case of the far less famous Reveillon riots in April 1789 in Faubourg St Anthoine. An unpopular manufacturer had threatened to lower wages. He was attacked at his factory, and 300 rioters were killed by troops.

  For the rest of the early period of the Revolution until 1792 there were very few deaths. Even in the vast peasant revolt of the summer of 1789 few nobles were actually killed. The peasants' anger was directed at property and documents.

  Source 19: The effects of the war were not only – and not even most importantly – effects on the King. All areas of French society were affected.

  The overthrow of the monarchy was not one of the original aims of the Revolution. Louis' overthrow is part of the radicalisation of the Revolution, another example of which is the extension of suffrage to all males.

✤✤✤

In other ways the Revolution is simply becoming more extreme. Violence is escalating and poverty increasing. It is a dangerous time.

ENQUIRY: WHY DID THE FRENCH EXECUTE THEIR KING?

Pupils' Book pp. 128–131
Worksheet 32

This two-spread enquiry looks at the charges against Louis and the nature of his trial. The pupils then have a chance to make a final judgement on him.

Worksheet 32 is a multiple choice quiz called 'Was Louis a good king?', which will reinforce pupils' grasp of the problems faced by Louis and how well he handled them. It parallels the quiz for Charles I (Worksheet 13). Comparisons can be drawn between the two, giving access to level 3 of AT1 strand c.

The actions that Louis actually took were 1c) (page 101), 2a) (page 114), 3b) (page 114), 4b) (page 115), 5a) (page 115), 6c) (page 117), 7a) (page 122), 8b) (page 126).

Pupils should be reminded that for their initial scoring they should ignore what Louis actually did. They can check their scoring against others' before looking back to Louis' actions. Their final score for Louis will reveal whether they think he made good decisions. The differences between the assessments made by different members of the class will be the stimulus for further class discussion of each of the options, in particular the opportunities Louis missed at the crucial moments in questions 5, 7 and 8.

Q1: AT1c level 2
Q2: AT3 levels 3, 4
Q3–4: AT3 levels 1, 3
Activity: AT1c levels 4, 5, AT3 level 4

Louis' trial

Question 1 allows you to make comparisons with a trial in Britain today. In discussing its fairness the fact that judge and jury were the same body is clearly significant.

The charges

Question 2: Give the pupils the following page references to assist their search:
■ bankrupting the nation, page 111
■ plotting against the Revolution, page 124
■ trying to flee, page 122
■ accepting a constitution he despised, page 126.

Do pupils regard these as good enough reasons to bring the King to trial? These days ousted leaders may be allowed to slip away unharmed, e.g. Eric Honecker of East Germany, or Ferdinand Marcos of the Philippines, as was James II of England (page 71).

Question 3: A = president, B = Louis, C = defence, D = prosecution, E = deputies.

The defence

Activity: This might be done in pairs, each person being asked to argue one side of the case. Once they have heard each point of view they could agree as a pair which side of the case they most support.

The verdict

For class discussion: Was the result of the trial close? And was the decision to execute Louis the right decision?

There was clearly little hesitation in finding the King guilty, but a lot of doubt about his fate.

Pupils might discuss whether the death penalty, as opposed to imprisonment, should only be acceptable where there is a unanimous verdict.

The voting itself was very complex. It took over 24 hours. Over 700 deputies publicly announced their vote. Many of them explained their decision with a speech.

All commentators simplify the complex results of the vote. The precise figures were: imprisonment/exile 288; reprieve 46; death with delay 26; immediate death 361.

Tension mounted as it became increasingly clear that the vote would be close. One deputy was brought in from his hospital bed. Every vote was crucial.

Summary Q1–4: AT1b levels 2, 3, 4, 5, 6, 7, AT1c levels 3, 4, 5

(Pages 130–131)
The emphasis here is on the human side of the story. We have also followed a similar format to the story of Charles' execution so that comparisons can be drawn.

The day before the execution: 20 January

Q1–2: AT1b level 2
Q3: AT2 level 7

The preparations

Q1: AT3 level 3
Q2: AT2 levels 4, 5, 6

The execution

Q1: AT3 levels 3, 4, 5, 6, 7
Q2: AT1c level 3, AT3 levels 3, 4
Q3: AT1b level 2
Q4: AT1b level 2, AT2 level 7, AT3 level 4

These events are similar to other occasions in history when a famous or dangerous prisoner has been moved. It would be very embarrassing and dangerous for anything to go wrong.

✠✠✠✠✠✠✠✠✠✠✠✠✠✠✠✠✠✠✠✠✠✠✠✠✠✠✠✠✠✠✠✠✠✠✠✠✠✠✠

Source 10: This comes from the Abbé Edgeworth, who travelled in the coach with Louis. He was obviously close to the action, but would be very sympathetic to the King. He left France in 1796 and spent the last ten years of his life in the service of the exiled heir to the throne.

The moments after the execution were bound to be a worry to the revolutionaries. Would there be a reaction to the execution? (The same worry caused the Bolsheviks in Russia to execute the Romanov royal family secretly at Ekaterinburg in 1918.) The evidence here seems to suggest they had few problems, although souvenir hunters were in evidence.

Source 12: The British, to promote their war effort and prevent revolutionary thoughts spreading to England, did not doubt the iniquity of the execution.

In **question 4** pupils will need to recap much of the evidence they have read in previous pages. You can direct them to pages 100–101, 111, 113–114, 122–131. Pupils are attempting to explain Louis' actions in terms of character and circumstances. They might well argue convincingly in favour of any of the three views of Louis.

There is considerable evidence of Louis' kind nature. He clearly states his desire to do the best for his country, though pupils should be encouraged to view such statements critically.

There is considerable evidence that Louis favoured what he saw as liberty. But for him it implied respect for authority, whereas he saw the Revolution degenerating into anarchy (Source 8 on page 124).

It is easy to see Louis as foolish. But many have concluded (as they have for Charles I) that more probably he was lacking the intelligence to respond effectively to rapidly changing circumstances.

ENQUIRY: WAS THE TERROR NECESSARY?

Pupils' Book pp. 132–137
Worksheets 33, 34

This three-spread enquiry investigates one of the most famous features of the Revolution – the Terror. The popular image is of pointless, even mindless, blood-letting. However, the Terror was in the first place a genuine attempt to respond to the crisis facing France.

(Pages 132–133)

Crisis

Q1: AT1b levels 2, 3, 4, 5, AT1c level 4

The Committee of Public Safety, with its strong authoritarian powers, was established to meet the crises facing France. By 1793 France was at war against most major countries in Europe. There was also a civil war. At the peak of the crisis over 60 departments were rejecting the Jacobin government in Paris. And yet there was growing popular pressure, in particular in the cities and

from the sans-culottes movement, to make the Revolution more radical still. There were major economic pressures, most notably rapid inflation, which provoked considerable popular unrest. This is the situation which we have attempted to summarise in Source 1.

In this context the Committee introduced measures to win the war and tribunals to deal with dissent, but also some positive ideas aiming to move the Revolution forward.

You might ask pupils what they understand by the term 'Terror'.

Other examples from world history of such emergency measures being taken can be referred to.

Question 1: To generate better pupil answers, discuss Sources 1–5 in class, and make a list of the problems.

Source 2: Discuss what the dangers of giving a small group so much power might be.

Source 4: Emphasise that this was a move to keep prices down. Pupils often perceive 'maximum' as implying the raising of prices.

Source 5: Conscription may need explaining. Pupils will have plenty of views on whether the *levée en masse* was a good idea. You might ask them what they think this order shows about the degree of desperation in the French war effort.

A new view of society

Q1: AT3 level 3
Q2: AT3 level 4

The Committee of Public Safety had two sides to its nature. On the one hand there are the harsh measures such as the Law of Suspects (Source 6). On the other there is the new advanced constitution of August 1793 which it helped bring in:

> ■ *The aim of Government is to do the best for all the people.*
> ■ *The country should help unfortunate citizens, either by providing them with work or by giving those unable to work enough to live on.*
> ■ *Education must be available for all citizens.*
> ■ *Don't do to others that which you wouldn't want done to you.*
> ■ *Every man over 25 years to vote.*

The new constitution, however, was almost immediately suspended.

The new calendar aimed to symbolise the break with the past. Mussolini tried the same thing. The introduction of the calendar formed an important part of the 'dechristianisation' movement of 1793–94, but also echoed government moves to metricate or decimalise everything. Pupils will have their own ideas on whether the new calendar had some good points and it should provoke an energetic class discussion.

The new calendar continued in use until 31 December 1806. Pupils might have some fun in suggesting problems, both within the country and in foreign relations, which this might bring.

A support activity: The new revolutionary calendar is about to be introduced. Write on the board these approximate English versions of the names of the months: Snowy, Showery, Blustery, Budding, Blooming, Growing, Plenteousness, Hotness, Fruitfulness, Harvest Time, Mist Time, Winter Time. Write a publicity note to be read out in every town square in France, explaining how the calendar will work and why it is an improvement on the old one.

The twelve months followed each other, then the five holidays were added in at the end (six in a leap year).

Pupils will have studied the new Islamic calendar (page 160 of *Contrasts and Connections*). That too was an attempt to break with the past and set up a new structure for time itself.

Question 1: The words on the cards are (from left to right): Spirit of War (strength); Freedom of Worship (fraternity); Equality of Duty (security); Spirit of the Arts (taste); Freedom of the Press (light); Equality of Ranks (power); Spirit of Peace (prosperity); Freedom of Marriage (modesty); Equality of Rights (justice); Wealth; Industry; Courage.

You could ask pupils to design their own playing card to encourage loyal revolutionaries.

Fear of Traitors

Q1: AT1c level 4, AT3 level 3
Activity: AT1c levels 4, 5, 6, 7

Question 1: To appreciate the dynamics of the tribunal do a detailed interrogation of Source 7. Who is the suspect? Why is the child there? Why is the man putting a piece of paper on the table? What does the paper say? Who is going to be doing the questioning? Who are the men on the right? Why are people pointing? Where will the suspect sit or stand? And so on.

You could also recreate the scene in a role-play.

Activity: The poster must make clear what practical steps ordinary people can take. Like all good advertising, to be effective the posters should concentrate on a few selected key points. Make a class display.

(Pages 134–135)

Who was executed and where?

Q1: AT3 level 3
Q2–3, 5–6: AT3 levels 3, 4
Q4: AT1b levels 2, 3, 4

The Terror is sometimes perceived to have involved mainly aristocrats and to have taken place mainly in Paris. The sources on this spread challenge these stereotypes.

Question 1: Constituents, legislature and convention are the three post-Revolutionary Assemblies.

Source 11: Although not as many nobles as peasants were executed, aristocratic victims formed a much higher proportion of their class than the peasants. Ask pupils why nobles' executions are remembered more than those of the peasants.

Source 12 quite clearly shows the regional nature of the Terror. This will be compared with a map showing areas of counter-revolution on page 140.

Question 6: It's not as easy as it might look. Pupils need to consider both Sources 9 and 12. You might also tell them that 70% of the deaths were in just five departments of France. However, as always, the way they support their answers from the sources is paramount.

The human tragedies

Q7: AT1c level 6

Sources 15 and 16 bring pupils back to appreciate the human tragedy of the Terror. The horror of past events is often best summed up in the experience of individuals rather than in the recounting of apparently horrendous figures. Pupils should consider whether Sources 15 and 16 or Source 9 give you a better impression of the horrors of the Terror.

(Pages 136–137)

Was the Terror necessary . . . ?

The aim of the spread as a whole is to set up the variety of opinions that can be expressed about the Terror, then and now. It is essentially an AT1c exercise with AT2 elements as we look at the differing perspectives of people today.

Look at Sources 17–19 together, then split into groups of three. Each person in the group is to summarise for the others in their group the main points in one of the remaining three colour panels.

. . . What outsiders said

Q1–2: AT3 levels 3, 4
Q3: AT3 levels 1, 3
Q4: AT1b level 2, AT1c level 6

. . . What French people said

Q1–2: AT3 level 3
Q3: AT1b levels 2, 3, AT1c level 7

Source 23: Pupils should bear in mind that the police might well exaggerate opposition to justify their existence.

. . . What modern historians have said

Q1: AT3 level 3
Q2–3: AT2 levels 2, 3, 4, 6, 7

✱✱

Question 3: Pupils can compare their own analysis of the Terror with those of recent historians.

You might ask them whether it matters that no French historian is represented in the extracts.

Activity: AT1c levels 4, 5, AT2 level 7

Activity: Worksheet 33 gives cue cards to help set up the debate. Copy them and cut them up so everyone can have one card and hand them out at random.

The aim of the debate is that pupils decide for themselves on a modern-day answer to this question. However, they need to hear evidence from the time as well as modern-day assessments.

First, ask two people who have concluded that the Terror was necessary to open the debate by reading out the paragraphs they have written. Then get two people who have concluded that it was unnecessary to do the same. (N.B. prepare your own paragraphs on each side, just in case the class is unanimous.)

Then call witnesses from the time, i.e. one person for each of the eight cards from Worksheet 33. You as chair or the class can question the witnesses.

Next, using the blackboard, draw up an overall list of reasons why the Terror was necessary and reasons why it was not. Include everyone's suggestions. Invite any summing up speeches people would like to make. Finally, take a class vote.

Worksheet 34 can also be cited as evidence on both sides – that the Terror worked to halt France's crisis, but that its escalation was unnecessary in that most executions happened after the crisis was past.

ENQUIRY: DID FRENCH PEOPLE SUPPORT THE REVOLUTION?

Pupils' Book pp. 138–143
Worksheets 34, 35

This is a three-spread enquiry which tackles a range of ideas across AT1 strand b and strand c. Pupils will need no reminding that people disagree about changes that take place around them – there are ample illustrations from everyday life.

(Pages 138–139)

The sans-culottes

Q1–2, 4–5: AT3 levels 1, 3
Q3: AT3 level 7
Q6: AT1c levels 4, 5, 6, 7
Q7: AT3 levels 3, 4, 5, 6
Q8: AT3 levels 3, 7
Q9 and Activity: AT1c levels 4, 5, 6, 7

Source 3: Compare the views of sans-culottes with those of the Diggers and the Levellers (pages 68–69).

(Pages 140–141)

Counter-revolution

Q1: AT3 levels 3, 4
Q2: AT1b level 2, AT1c levels 6, 7

Question 1: overlays on a OHP might help here.

Who were the counter-revolutionaries?

Q1: AT1b level 2, AT1c levels 6, 7
Q2: AT1c levels 4, 5, 6
Q3: AT1b level 2, AT1c levels 7, 8, 9
Q4: AT1a levels 3, 4, 5, 6, 7

Worksheet 35 provides a fascinating poem that conveys some of the counter-revolutionary feeling. Pupils read across the page to start with, then fold it lengthways and reach each half down the page for a very different message.

(Pages 142–143)

The murder of Marat

Q1: AT1b level 2
Q2a): AT3 level 3
Q2b): AT1c level 6
Q3: AT1b level 4
Activity: AT1b levels 2, 3, 4, 5, AT1c levels 4, 5, 6, 7, AT3 level 4

The previous two spreads focused on reactions of groups of people to the Revolution. This one focuses on two individuals, although the spread also brings out the clash between the radical Jacobins and moderate Girondins.

The emphasis is on the consequences – intended and unintended – of Marat's assassination, so one strategy for using this spread is to keep the outcome of the events a mystery to start with. Don't have the pupils' book open. Tell the story yourself as far as Charlotte Corday's execution. Then ask pupils to say what they expect to be the results of Marat's assassination. Will the Terror get worse or lessen? And why? How will the Jacobins respond to the assassination of one of their leaders?

Then turn to the pupils' book. The questions taken together focus on the consequence side of AT1 strand b.

Worksheet 34 – the Terror timeline – can be used again at this point to locate the assassination in the context of the Terror. The timeline also raises the problematic links between the extent of the Terror and the extent of the crisis facing France. Pupils can easily see how the killings got out of hand. Maximum Terror did *not* coincide with the maximum crisis.

Question 2 will reveal how much pupils have understood of the situation of the Jacobins and attitudes towards them.

Look very carefully at the painting, together with the description of how it was created. It will be almost

❀❀

essential to discuss in class a little more about what a martyr is, and how revolutionary propaganda could have used 'martyr' images.

Ask pupils what they think the note is in Marat's hand. Corday's note? Or his own? It is actually the note Corday wrote for Marat. It says: 'Marat. It is enough that I am unhappy that I have the right to your kindness.' But what does that mean?

Pupils could also be asked to imagine what the note that Corday carried on her to explain her motives might say, and write it down.

Question 4 is another citizenship question.

ENQUIRY: ROBESPIERRE: HERO OR VILLAIN?

Pupils' Book pp. 144–145

This is a single-spread enquiry that closes Section 3 and bridges the gap into Section 4 on Napoleon.

The main aim is to focus on AT2. The heading sums up two extreme views of Robespierre. Through the sources pupils can see how both views can be supported. They can also form their own opinion – though necessarily a provisional one.

Q1: AT3 levels 1, 3
Q3–4: AT1b levels 2, 3, 4, AT1c level 6
Q5–6: AT2 levels 2, 3, 4, 5, 6, 8
Q7–8: AT1c levels 4, 5, 6, 7, AT2 levels 6, 7, AT3 levels 3, 4

Question 1: Get pupils to concentrate on the picture to start with in making their list of words.

Question 2: Source 2 raises the question of whether violence can be justified in a good cause. Most pupils will have a view on this, whether applied to the playground, animal rights or international terrorism. A discussion of such issues is in our opinion a vital component of citizenship education.

Source 6: There are other cartoons with similar messages on pages 96 and 134 of the pupils' book.

Question 7: Gather pupils' views together in an overall list on the blackboard. Some guidance on the positives might be helpful. Remind pupils about what they have seen of the role of Robespierre both in the Terror and in solving some of France's biggest problems in 1793–94.

Some comparisons can be drawn with Cromwell (see Activity on page 67).

Section 4: How did Napoleon change France and Europe?

The next five enquiries investigate the Napoleonic Era. We have not dealt with it in the depth given to the Revolution itself. Our main interest in this section is to compare the changes of the Revolution with the changes brought about by Napoleon.

ENQUIRY: COUP D'ETAT!

Pupils' Book pp. 146–149
Worksheet 36

A two-spread enquiry, with the emphasis in the questions on AT3 work and on causation.

The timescale has now changed. Refer pupils back to the timeline on pages 94–95 (Worksheet 24). After thirty pages or more on the events of a few years, this single enquiry takes us through fifteen years.

(Pages 146–147)

France in 1799

Q1: AT3 levels 1, 3
Q2: AT1b levels, 2, 3, 4, AT1c level 6
Q3: AT1b levels 2, 3, AT3 levels 3, 4

Question 1 is best done in pairs. Napoleon showed astuteness in not getting involved in the messy Vendean civil wars, but many commentators have emphasised the role of luck in his rise to power. Luck can sometimes be a significant cause of historical events.

Question 2: Pupils will need to refer back to the bulleted points in the first column. They can also note the similarities to the situation facing France in 1793 (Source 1 on page 132). That was only six years earlier and the memory of that crisis would not have died.

There are citizenship opportunities here as well. Why is it that coups seem so often to succeed? *Coups d'état* are common and there might be recent ones that you can refer to. Do pupils feel that a coup can be justified as a way of stabilising a country?

Worksheet 36 can be used at this point to help pupils place the events of the previous decade in chronological order.

(Pages 148–149)

The coup

Q1–3: AT3 levels 3, 4
Q4: AT3 levels 5, 6, 7

Question 1: Use a grid like this to record pupils' views on the various versions:

	Source 5	Source 6	Source 7
Napoleon			
Council members			

Question 4: Napoleon of course sanctioned Source 4, which is very partial to him. Source 5, on the other hand, is written well after the event by someone closely

involved but who was not initially free to record his memories. Sources 6 and 7 are also partisan.

The Emperor

Q1: AT3 levels 3, 4
Q2–4: AT1b levels 2, 3, 4

Some comparisons can be made here with Cromwell being offered the English crown (page 67).

Detailed interrogation of Sources 8 and 9 will be needed.

ENQUIRY: DID NAPOLEON BETRAY THE REVOLUTION?

Pupils' Book pp. 150–153
Worksheets 37, 38

A two-spread enquiry, with work mainly based around the chart on pages 150–151, this enquiry addresses a central question for the unit as a whole. It contrasts the changes brought about by the Revolution in 1789–93 with the changes brought about by Napoleon.

Although the logic of reading has required us to put the two spreads of the enquiry in this order, with the chart followed by the information needed to complete it, that is not the order in which they should be used. Pages 152–153 (bar the final activity) should be fully discussed in class before pupils fill out the chart on page 151. It's the quality of classroom discussion around the issues on pages 152–153 that will determine how interesting this enquiry will be.

(Pages 150–151)

Changes

Activity: AT1a levels 3, 4, 5, 6, 7, AT1c levels 4, 5

Write up Source 1 big and bold on the blackboard. It is the claim to measure Napoleon's actions against.

Our suggestions for the completed final column are as follows:
- All laws reorganised into a single simplified system, the Code Napoleon
- Napoleon imprisons people he considers dangerous. Over 2500 people are imprisoned without trial for political offences
- Napoleon censors and closes down newspapers
- Napoleon says education should be mainly for men
- Napoleon finally establishes state schools
- Any religion is allowed but Catholicism is 'officially approved'
- Bishops are appointed by Napoleon, and have to make an oath to support the government
- The Church is paid for by the state
- The Church does not get back its lands that were sold off

- Napoleon guarantees that feudalism will never return
- Napoleon creates new titles, but the new nobles have no special privileges.

Worksheet 37 is a copy of the chart for pupils to fill in. The information they need is largely on pages 152–153. There may be too much research and reading for pupils to do on their own, so here are some strategies for differentiation:
- give line references for the information pupils need
- fill in the majority of the boxes in the context of the class discussion around pages 152–153
- ask pupils which topic they are most interested in and would like to research.

(Pages 152–153)

Q1–6: AT1c level 2
Activity: AT1a levels 3, 4, 5, 6, AT1b level 2, AT1c levels 6, 7

Questions 1–5 are designed for class discussion. They should precede work on the chart on pages 150–151. Discussion about each category could be carried out in smaller study groups.

We shouldn't expect pupils to get interested in civil service reform, but some of the other issues have great potency today, and they raise many issues for citizenship education.

Source 3, for instance, with its authoritarian model for family life and other institutions, prompts the question of whether this is what a family, or a school, needs today.

Individual rights

We have studied the Declaration of the Rights of Man in some detail (pages 118–121). Many of these fundamental rights were suspended under the Terror. So Napoleon was not breaking with the practice of the Revolution, even if he was breaking with the ideals.

Discuss with pupils statements A and B in Source 4. Why should Napoleon have believed this? Does the government have any control over the press today? How is the government's propaganda (or the opposition's for that matter) spread? Do they need the newspapers or the bishops to spread their message? Are there times when censorship is justified and times when it is not? Refer pupils back to Napoleon's propagandist poster describing the *Coup de Brumaire* (page 147).

Detention without trial remains an issue in civil rights, most notably, in Britain, in the context of combating terrorism. The call for internment regularly resurfaces in debating solutions to the terrorist problem in Northern Ireland.

Education

Education is a live political issue in the 1990s. Napoleon's education system was essentially elitist, in that it was designed to cream off the best pupils and train them into public service, even if it was also public and free. Does this echo aspects of education policy today? Are our schools designed to educate everybody or just to cream off the best?

In looking at statement D in Source 4, which will doubtless surface in many pupils' choices for **question 6**, you can take the discussion further by asking pupils to consider whether they think this statement might have been more reasonable in the early 1800s than it is today, and why. This will raise a heated debate in any classroom. Should men be taught different things to women? Is there sex stereotyping in subject choice and treatment today?

Question 4: In practice, you might wish to combine discussion of this question with the wider opportunities presented by question 6.

The Catholic Church

This raises the question of whether the state should have an official religion. In Britain Christianity receives preferential treatment to other religions: this can be demonstrated in the bias towards Christianity of the blasphemy laws.

Thus RE in schools is mainly Christian, and schools or children of other faiths have to 'opt out' of this if they wish. The Christian consensus is assumed, and the government's justification remains that Christianity is the religion of the majority – an echo of the Napoleonic era.

Peasants and nobles

One art of politics is keeping most of the people happy. Pupils can consider how minorities can lose out by this. Who specifically might have lost out in Napoleon's France by this policy?

Question 6: Discussion will bring out many of these themes. You could handle question 6 as a secret ballot. Pupils write their choice on a card. Collect the cards and establish which is the statement most agreed with and which the least. Focus class discussion on the top and bottom statements.

The statements themselves raise some additional issues concerning the role of women and democracy, both areas where Napoleon appears to have set back the revolutionary advances, though pupils may have differing views on how much the Revolution had advanced in these areas anyway.

The game on **Worksheet 38** attempts to document the fortunes of women and their contributions to the Revolution. Enlarge it to A3 size. You will need one copy for every three pupils. Read the playing instructions on the worksheet carefully.

One pupil in each group should be middle class, one an urban worker and one a peasant. Each square in the game indicates whether it applies to the peasants, the urban workers or the middle classes. Pupils must keep a record of their score after each throw. If they die, of course, they drop out of the game.

The main point of a game such as this is to provoke discussion.

■ Investigate how the pupils fared in each round. When did they make progress (i.e. gain points) and when not?
■ Do pupils agree with the scores on the squares? They might like to white out the scores and create a new set of scores that reflect their own views of which were the greatest steps forwards or the worst steps backwards.
■ Games simplify history. What events or factors that would have influenced women's lives have been left out?

Activity: So far the spread has been approaching Napoleon's reforms from a more modern perspective. Now pupils are in role, and trying to see the changes through the eyes of a character from the time.

Other characters could be chosen, e.g. a Girondin or a sans-culottes.

To start with, pupils should consider which of the changes might affect their character. The next stage is to establish what their character might have thought of the changes.

The fullest answers will also attempt to express the character's views on changes that may not directly have affected them.

ENQUIRY: NAPOLEON: THE FIRST EUROPEAN?

Pupils' Book pp. 154–155
Worksheet 39

This single-spread enquiry focuses on AT1 strand a, and on how Napoleon changed Europe. It also forms a useful context in which to look at some of the issues of European integration that confront us in Britain today.

Q1: AT3 levels 1, 3
Q2: AT2 level 4

Question 1: It might be worth writing Sources 1–3 on the board at the start of the lesson and keeping the pupils' book closed, so that the conflicting perspective offered by Sources 4–8 does not get in the way.

Question 2 also focuses on a specific idea within AT2: how choice of evidence can determine interpretation.

The Continental System

Q1, 3: AT1a levels 3, 4
Q2: AT1a level 7
Q4: AT1a levels 5, 6

The Continental System was almost impossible to enforce. Pupils will know how difficult it is to control smuggling even today, e.g. in the drugs trade.

Worksheet 39 is a larger version of the map on page 154. It shows the areas controlled by Napoleon in 1810. Pupils can use Source 9 and colour code the map to show how great an impact Napoleon's changes would have had

✤✤

in each country. Four degrees of impact are given on the worksheet, but question 3 will have suggested that all of Europe was affected to some extent. If pupils include some countries in the 'no impact' category, there will be an opportunity to discuss this further.

ENQUIRY: WHY WAS NAPOLEON DEFEATED?

Pupils' Book pp. 156–163
Worksheet 40

There are two main strands running through this four-spread enquiry.

The first is a causation strand, approached through the story of Napoleon's defeat – including detailed study of the Spanish and Russian campaigns.

The second is an examination of Britain's role in the defeat – approached essentially as an AT2 exercise.

(Pages 156–157)
Source 1: This can be used later on, in the Activity on page 165, at which stage it should be interrogated in detail.

Trafalgar

Q1a): AT3 levels 3,4
Q1c): AT1b level 2, AT1c level 6
Q2: AT3 levels 3, 4, 5, 6

Question 1b): The story of David and Goliath.
Question 2: Pupils will have to speculate on the effects on the French.

Britain's role in Napoleon's defeat

Q1: AT2 levels 5, 6, 7

(Pages 158–159)
The Peninsular War

Q1–2: AT3 levels 3, 4

Sources 8 and 9: Most of the series of etchings and paintings – some of them quite brutal – can be seen in Gwyn Williams' book *Goya and the Impossible Revolution*, published by Penguin/Alan Lane.

Guerrilla Warfare

Q1: AT1c levels 4, 5
Q2: AT1b levels 3, 4, 5
Activity: AT1b levels 3, 4, 5, 6, 7, 8, 9

Guerrilla is Spanish for 'little war'. Guerrilla warfare is something that pupils are going to come across

repeatedly – particularly in their study of twentieth-century history – and this spread can help lay foundations for these later studies.

Question 1: Pupils can work in threes, writing one entry each.
Activity: Pupils can be asked to write another version of the report, which *will* be seen by Napoleon.

(Pages 160–161)

Disaster in Russia

Source 14: Emphasise the sheer scale of Russia – the march from the river Niemen to Moscow is 1100 kilometres.

The retreat from Moscow

Q1: AT1b levels 3, 4, 5, 6, 7
Q2: AT1b level 6
Activity: AT1c levels 5, 6, 7

Question 1: Pupils can work on two or three of these categories.
Activity: This could be a letter home, or a diary, or an official log – pupils can choose. There will be interesting comparisons to be made between the versions.

(Pages 162–163)

The final defeat

Q1: AT2 level 5
Activity: AT1b levels 4, 5, AT2 level 5

This account of the final defeat is told very sparsely – you may wish to tell the story yourself with more elaboration.

Question 1 returns to an AT2 theme. The dates at which the various labelled places were built or named is approximately:
- Trafalgar Square and Nelson's Column: 1829–43
- Waterloo Place: 1816
- Waterloo Station: 1848

On the road southwards out of London there is a series of churches built in the 1820s called the Waterloo churches. All are identical in construction and all are built at an important road junction. They are at Waterloo itself, Kennington (opposite the Oval station), Brixton and Norwood.

It is possible to pick up citizenship issues here as well as doing some local history. The naming and renaming of parks, streets and public buildings, and the building of statues, fountains and other memorials has a clear education and/or propaganda role, whether it be naming streets after military heroes or parks after civil rights leaders.

Pupils can do an assessment of their own local area – are there any Wellington, Waterloo, Trafalgar or Nelson names, memorials or statues in their home town? Use the index of your local map book.

In some places memorials were built in pairs – one for Waterloo or Wellington, another for Trafalgar or Nelson. Pupils should try and find out the dates that these local memorials were set up and who was responsible for them. In that way it is possible to track the Nelson and Wellington legend through the nineteenth century.

Napoleon's health

Q1–2: AT1b levels 2, 3
Q3: AT1b levels 2, 3, 4
Activity: AT1b levels 2, 3, 4, 5, AT1c levels 4, 5, 6, 7, AT2 levels 4, 5

This exercise is only generally related to Napoleon's defeat, but pupils seem to enjoy looking at this medical case history and, equally importantly, the wounds and diseases form a very tangible record of Napoleon's career. His victories and defeats can quite literally be read on his body. This exercise therefore helps to review Napoleon's career as a background for the obituary activity.

Answers to **questions 1–3** concerning the role of his medical problems in his defeat are necessarily tentative, but can provoke vigorous discussion.

N.B. A slow heart beat is not a bad thing to have, of course.

Activity: make comparisons between the obituaries.

As far as the choice of sources to illustrate the obituary goes, there are fifteen to choose from on pages 146–165. It could be a picture of Napoleon himself, a picture from his wars, a cartoon, a statue, or an artefact such as the proclamation.

The comparison between the obituaries will be most marked in the choice of illustrative visuals.

Comparisons with Cromwell are also possible at this point, and **Worksheet 40** can be used here. It lists some of the similarities and differences, and you may wish to introduce others, e.g. were they both 'dictators'?

ENQUIRY: HOW HAS NAPOLEON BEEN VIEWED THROUGH HISTORY?

Pupils' Book pp. 164–165

This is a single-spread enquiry focusing on AT2. It looks very briefly at the Napoleon legend. It needs to be read alongside the subsequent enquiry on the legacy of the French Revolution, which includes work on the legacy of Napoleon.

Q1: AT3 level 3

Question 1: The symbols are:
■ injured France – the maimed eagle which forms his hat
■ victims – the bodies that make up his face and the sea of blood for his collar
■ watchful allies – the spider.

The legend of Napoleon

Q2–3: AT3 levels 3, 4
Q4: AT3 levels 3, 4, 5, 7
Q5: AT2 levels 8, 9

Conclusions

Q6: AT2 levels 4, 5, 6
Activity: AT2 levels 5, 6, 7, 8, 9

Use the quotes at the top of the page as a basis for class discussion. Pupils may need to have the context of some of the quotes explained.

Activity: A collection of adverts on video and from magazines would obviously be helpful here. We've seen Napoleon brandy, travel agents (not getting stuck in Russia!) and numerous references to Napoleon's size (personal computers, small business advisers).

To prime pupils' imagination bring in a few sample products they could try to advertise: shampoo, a fashion garment, a camera, etc.

ENQUIRY: THE LEGACY OF THE FRENCH REVOLUTION

Pupils' Book pp. 166–169
Worksheets 41, 42

A two-spread enquiry geared towards AT1 strand b (examining the long-term consequences of the Revolution and of Napoleon) and AT2 (looking at the way the Revolution has been interpreted through history).

With some classes you may choose to use only the first spread, which concentrates on the more concrete aspects of the legacy.

(Pages 166–167)

The Revolution lives on

Activity: AT1a levels 3, 4, 5, 6, 7, AT1b levels 4, 5, 6, 7

Activity: Differentiation can be achieved by isolating two or three frames of the cartoon to focus on.

The Legion of Honour is a complex system of honours and awards which covers similar ground to Britain's honours system (e.g. MBEs and knighthoods) but has military divisions as well.

The Code Napoleon: French law is still based on it to the extent that it established:
■ one set of laws for the whole of France rather than different provincial laws
■ one law for all classes
■ the basic outline of today's civil law, family law, commercial law and criminal law.

Obviously, individual laws have changed, e.g. the right of a father to imprison his child for one month.

✿✿

The *Marseillaise*: the words in translation are:
Over us the bloodstained banner
Of tyranny holds sway.
Do you hear in the countryside
The roar of those fierce soldiers?
To arms, citizens!
Form your battalions;
March on, march on,
So that their tainted blood
Should drench our fields.

The following extracts from an article in *Time* magazine (March 1992) show that the debate about the Revolution's legacy continues. It appeared under the headline *Meddling with the* Marseillaise: *a proposal to bowdlerise France's barn-burning anthem provokes an indignant* Mon Dieu! *from traditionalists.*

❝ *. . . Today the song's robust words, which enjoin the children of revolutionary France to 'drench our fields' with the 'tainted blood' of the enemy, are under siege by those who feel the piece smacks of political incorrectness.*

French human rights advocate Abbé Pierre called for the song to be altered from 'words of hate to a message of love'.

Proposed changes:

Liberty, dearest Liberty,
Your bloody ramparts have fallen.
To be French, Ah! what luck!
Let's be proud of our flag . . .

Together, citizens,
Let us march hand in hand.
Sing on, sing on,
So that our songs
Silence all cannons.

Traditionalists are now rallying against the meddlers, denouncing the notion of tampering with the song that rang through the torchlit streets of revolutionary France as nothing short of traitorous. ❞

The relevance of the *Marseillaise* to freedom movements in the twentieth century has also been proved: it was sung by the protesters in Tiananmen Square, Beijing, before the massacre there in 1989.

Lenin: Other revolutions owed a similar debt to the ideals of the French Revolution. Indeed, as the next spread illustrates, the ideals of liberty, fraternity and equality were the rallying cry for European revolutions throughout the nineteenth century.

Some commentators suggest that the ideals of the Revolution were even more powerful a slogan in the Russia of 1989 than in the Russia of 1917 (see Gorbachev quote on page 169).

The Arc de Triomphe: Interestingly enough, work was suspended on the Arc on Napoleon's abdication, then restarted in 1824 to boost French nationalism.

It names all Napoleon's victories. Comparison can be made with the picture of London on page 162.

Martello Towers: There are 103 of these along the southern and eastern coasts of England. They were built by the government between 1805 and 1812.

The *Tricolore* was made up of the white of the royal family surrounded by the red and blue of Paris. Nowadays, we see a tricolour as almost the norm for a flag. Pupils need to see that the French invented it.

The flags shown are of the following countries: France, Ireland, Italy, Germany, Mexico, Belgium, India, Iran, Ethiopia, Ghana, Hungary. These countries all achieved independence in the nineteenth and twentieth centuries.

(Pages 168–169)

The nineteenth century

The twin concepts of democracy and nationalism lie behind these developments in Europe.

Democracy – rule by the people – has been covered extensively in this unit. Nationalism has not.

The Revolution and Napoleon together launched this new force into the world: the desire of people of the same race, beliefs, culture or language to be united and independent and to form political units of their own. It was France's wars, in particular, which strengthened nationalism in Europe.

In June 1794 the foreign invasions of France had been beaten back by the revolutionary army and the French armies moved onto the attack. Over the next twenty years they conquered much of Europe. The defeated countries began to discover their own national characters in their resistance to France.

Pupils will be able to see from Source 1 how the boundaries and names are in some places close to modern European ones, while in others they are not. Many of the boundaries cut across what we would now regard as natural cultural or ethnic divisions.

There will be ample examples of the continuing power of nationalism to refer to.

The twentieth century

Q1: AT2 levels 2, 3, 4, 5, 6, 7, 8, 9, 10
Activity: AT1b levels 4, 5, 6

Question 1: The quotes are: Goebbels – Source 5; Gorbachev – Source 4; Thatcher – Source 3.

Activity: You can use **Worksheet 41** to help you do your own class survey. Ask pupils to choose the two most important results of the French Revolution. Write the list of results on the board, and then find out how many people have put each result in their top two. Question 3 is for class discussion.

Worksheet 42 draws some comparisons between the English and French Revolutions.

Timeline: The French Revolution

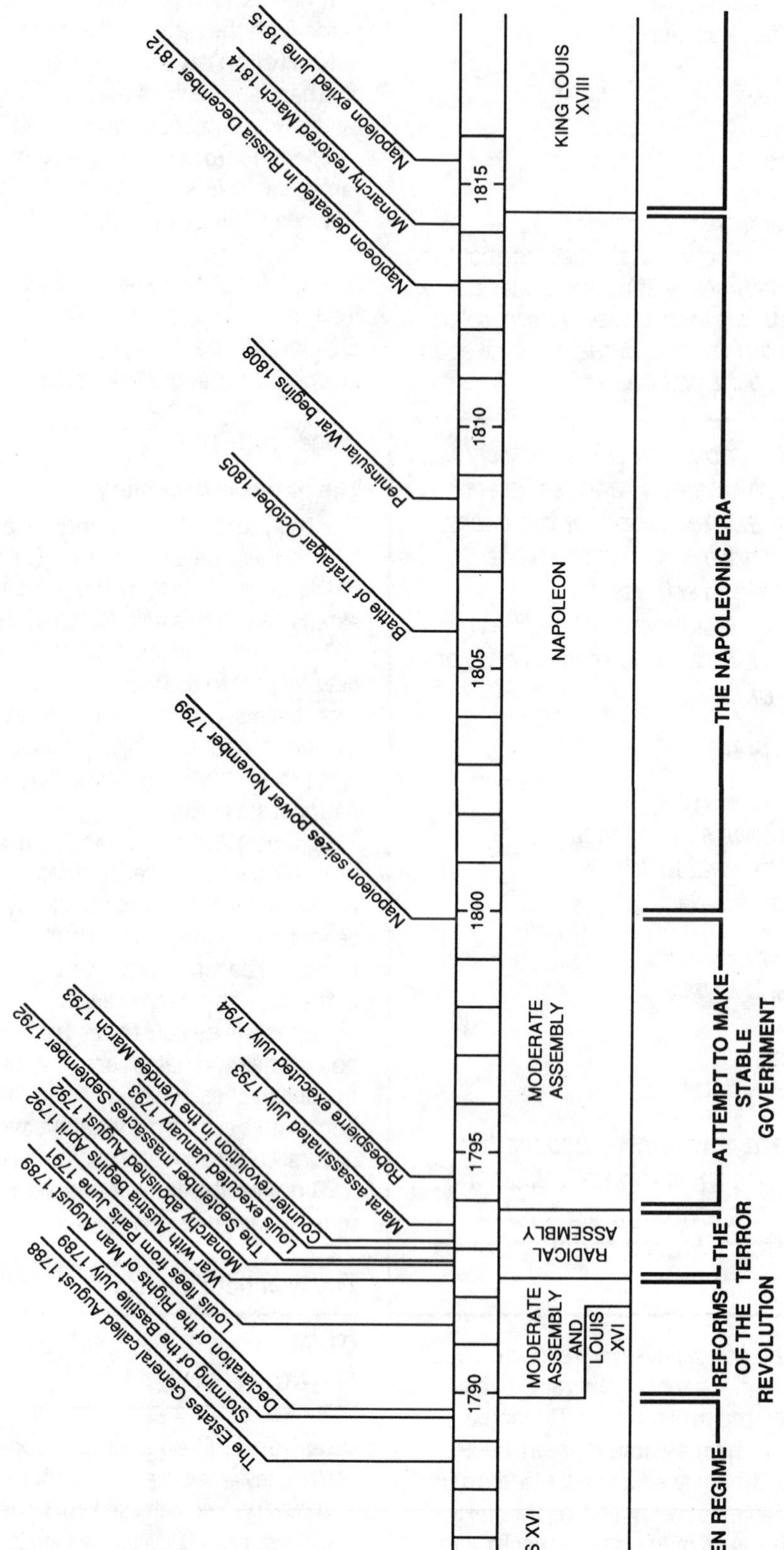
EVENTS
DATE
WHO RULED FRANCE?
1785
1790
1795
1800
1805
1810
1815
The Estates General called August 1788
Storming of the Bastille July 1789
Declaration of the Rights of Man August 1789
Louis flees from Paris June 1791
War with Austria begins April 1792
Monarchy abolished August 1792
The September massacres September 1792
Louis executed January 1793
Counter revolution in the Vendee March 1793
Marat assassinated July 1793
Robespierre executed July 1794
Napoleon seizes power November 1799
Battle of Trafalgar October 1805
Peninsular War begins 1808
Napoleon defeated in Russia December 1812
Monarchy restored March 1814
Napoleon exiled June 1815
LOUIS XVI
MODERATE ASSEMBLY AND LOUIS XVI
RADICAL ASSEMBLY
MODERATE ASSEMBLY
NAPOLEON
KING LOUIS XVIII
THE ANCIEN REGIME
REFORMS OF THE REVOLUTION
THE TERROR
ATTEMPT TO MAKE STABLE GOVERNMENT
THE NAPOLEONIC ERA

Paris

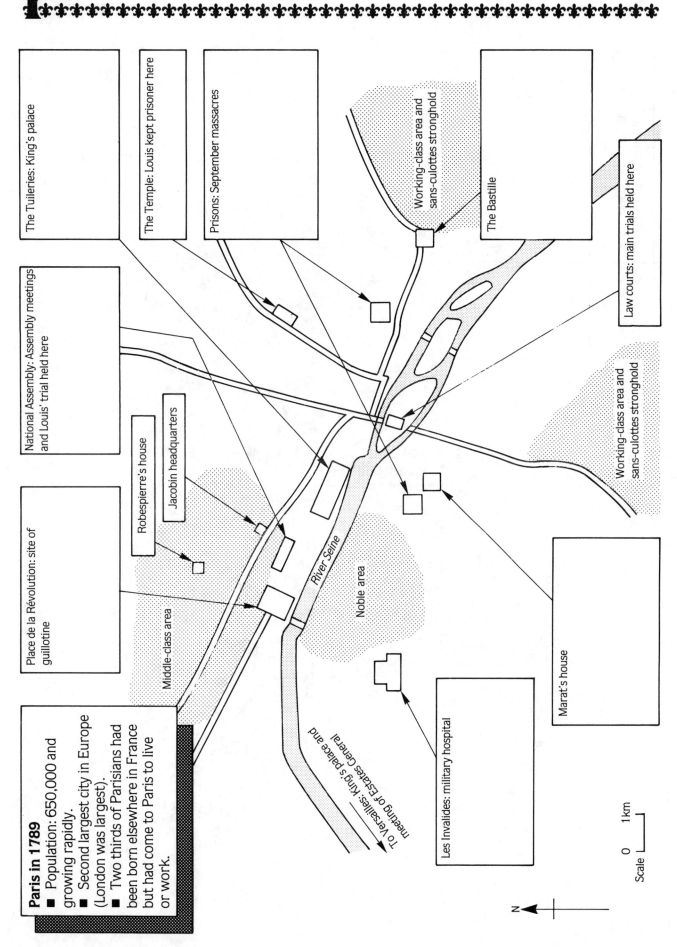

Paris in 1789
- Population: 650,000 and growing rapidly.
- Second largest city in Europe (London was largest).
- Two thirds of Parisians had been born elsewhere in France but had come to Paris to live or work.

The Tuileries: King's palace

The Temple: Louis kept prisoner here

Prisons: September massacres

Working-class area and sans-culottes stronghold

The Bastille

Law courts: main trials held here

National Assembly: Assembly meetings and Louis' trial held here

Robespierre's house

Jacobin headquarters

Working-class area and sans-culottes stronghold

Place de la Révolution: site of guillotine

Middle-class area

River Seine

Noble area

Marat's house

Les Invalides: military hospital

To Versailles: king's palace and meeting of Estates General

N

Scale
0   1km

The storming of the Bastille

✳✳

Write your own labels onto this picture to show the events mentioned in question 1 on page 98 of your book.

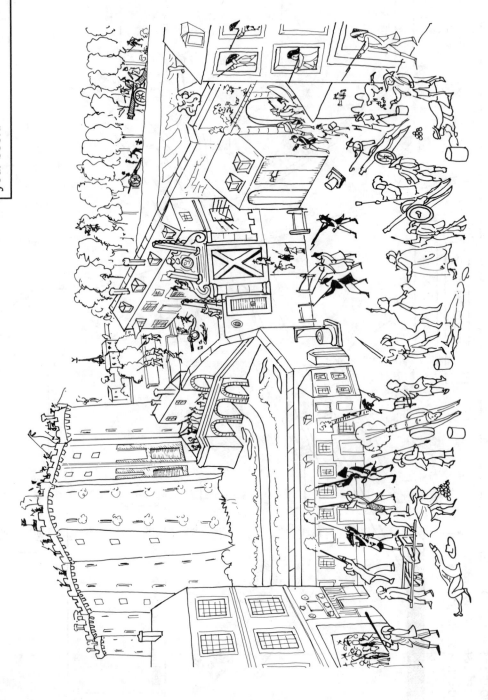

90

France before the Revolution

1. Add notes or drawings to this diagram to show the problems faced by members of each of the three estates.
2. The king had problems too. After you have studied pages 110–112 add notes or drawings to show the problems faced by the king.

Remember: the further down the pyramid people are, the poorer they are.

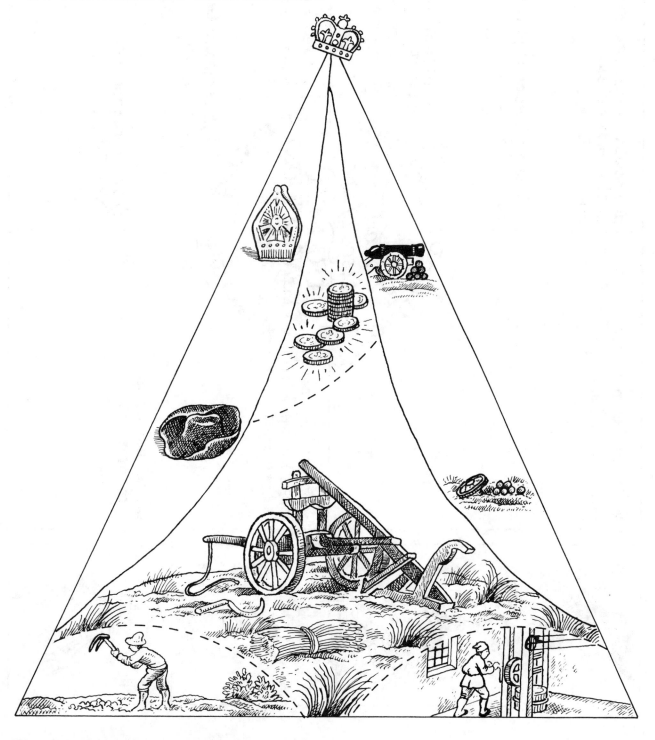

Long-term causes of the French Revolution

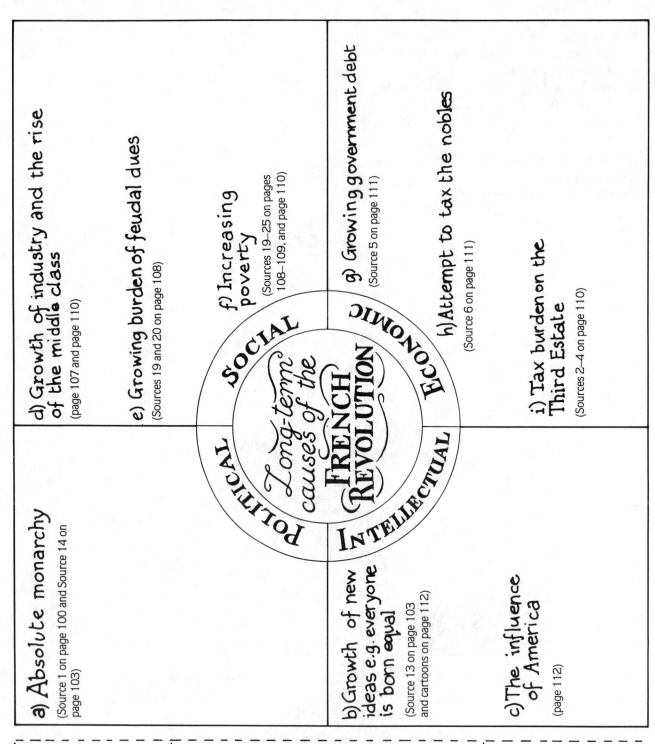

Long-term causes of the FRENCH REVOLUTION

SOCIAL

d) Growth of industry and the rise of the middle class
(page 107 and page 110)

e) Growing burden of feudal dues
(Sources 19 and 20 on page 108)

f) Increasing poverty
(Sources 19–25 on pages 108–109, and page 110)

ECONOMIC

g) Growing government debt
(Source 5 on page 111)

h) Attempt to tax the nobles
(Source 6 on page 111)

i) Tax burden on the Third Estate
(Sources 2–4 on page 110)

POLITICAL

a) Absolute monarchy
(Source 1 on page 100 and Source 14 on page 103)

INTELLECTUAL

b) Growth of new ideas e.g. everyone is born equal
(Source 13 on page 103 and cartoons on page 112)

c) The influence of America
(page 112)

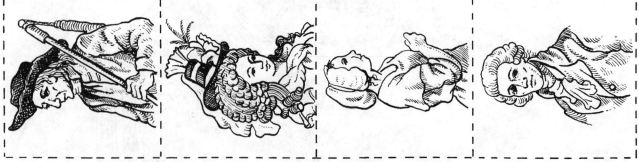

The trouble with France is . . .

It is February 1789. You have to interview each of these characters to find out what they think is wrong with France, or what problems are making them unhappy at the moment.

Fill in the word bubbles to show what they might say.

Remember to make sure they say *why* they are unhappy as well as saying what they are unhappy about.

Peasant
- Lives in a small run-down cottage.
- Pays one quarter of all harvest to two nobles.
- Has two sons who have gone to Paris to try to find work now that times are hard.

Middle-class businessman
- Lives in Paris in a large town house.
- Owns the warehouse in Source 17 on page 107.

Urban worker
- Lives in Lyon, a leading textile town (see page 107).
- Her whole family work in the textile industry.

Noblewoman
- Lives in a large chateau (like the one in Source 1 on page 106).
- From one of the richest families in France, who own a new ironworks in northern France.
- Has a brother who has fought in the American War of Independence (see page 112).

Which revolution?

✦✦

Look at these pictures. Some of the events and developments shown are causes of the English Revolution. Some are causes of the French Revolution. Some are causes of both. For each one say which revolution it helped cause.

There are two blank boxes. In these draw in two more causes and say which revolution they apply to.

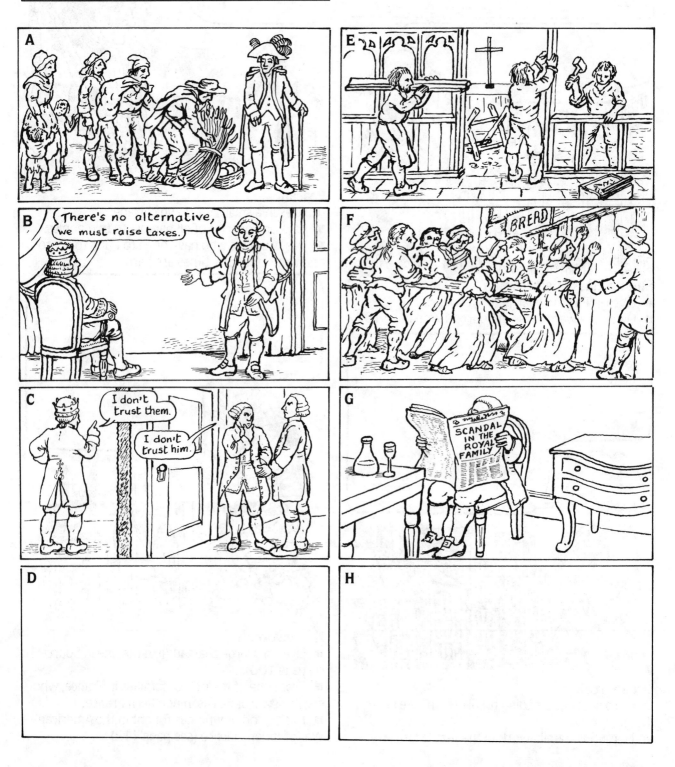

The royal family escapes

✦✦

❦ THE NEWS ❦

22ND JUNE 1791

Was Louis a good king?

You are going to judge how good a king Louis was.

Work in pairs. Look at the problems on this sheet and the possible actions Louis could take to deal with each one.

You probably remember what Louis actually did, but forget that for the time being. Imagine you are advising Louis in the eighteenth century.

For each problem, decide which of the actions would be most sensible (give that action three points) and which would be least sensible (give that one point). The remaining action gets two points.

1. It is 1784. A book has been published spreading rumours that Marie Antoinette spends too much money and has many lovers. Should Louis:
   a) publicly condemn her and get a divorce *or*
   b) do nothing and hope the rumours will go away *or*
   c) ban the book and burn all the copies?

2. It is 1788. The government is bankrupt and needs to raise more money. Should Louis:
   a) call a meeting of representatives from all of France to discuss how to raise more money *or*
   b) spend less and sell off some of his belongings *or*
   c) borrow more money?

3. It is 1788. Many French people are unhappy with the way France is being run. Should Louis:
   a) resign *or*
   b) ask each village and town to submit a complaint to him about what is wrong with France *or*
   c) tell his critics they should go and live somewhere else if they don't like France?

4. It is May 1789. Louis has called a meeting of the Estates General, for the first time since 1614. The representatives have gathered for the meeting in Versailles. But Louis' son is dying of tuberculosis. Should he:
   a) send his apologies and tell them to get on without him *or*
   b) go to the debates, even though he will find it hard to concentrate *or*
   c) adjourn the meeting for a few weeks?

5. The Estates General are unhappy that Louis seems to be doing nothing about France's problems. They vow not to go home until France has been given a constitution that makes everyone equal. Should Louis:
   a) use troops to send the Estates General home *or*
   b) suggest a delay of a year to look into the possibility of a new constitution *or*
   c) tell them he thinks their ideas are good and he would like to see the draft constitution next week?

6. It is October 1789. Thousands of women want to take Louis to Paris so that he will be more in touch with what is going on there. Should Louis:
   a) order his troops to disperse the women *or*
   b) ask the women to stay with him instead *or*
   c) go back with them to Paris?

7. It is 1791. The King and his family are trapped in the Tuileries Palace in Paris. Louis doesn't like the changes the Revolution is making. Should he:
   a) try to escape and seek the support of foreign countries to fight against the Revolution *or*
   b) suggest a referendum to see if most people in France support the changes *or*
   c) send his family to freedom in another country but stay in Paris himself?

8. It is 1792. France is at war with Austria. Things are going badly. It looks as if France will lose. Should Louis:
   a) take charge of the army to fight in the war against the Austrians *or*
   b) send secret letters to the Austrians asking their help to restore his power *or*
   c) send posters to every town and village encouraging them to join the war effort?

Once you have scored each set of actions look in your book or find out from your teacher what Louis actually did. Then add up his score, according to the points you have given each action.

8–13: You think Louis was a pretty awful king.
14–19: You think Louis made a lot of mistakes but tried his best.
20–24: You think Louis was a brilliant king.

Compare the score you have given Louis with the score that other members of the class have given him. Do you disagree? If you do, find out why. Have you scored the actions differently?

Dreadful but necessary

Teacher:
Copy and cut up the following statements. Hand them out to different members of the class to get the debate going.

REVOLUTIONARY LEADER
(You believe the Terror is dreadful but necessary)

"People who resist the Revolution are like a cancer inside France. We must cut the cancer out before it starts to grow. Otherwise the Revolution will die."

JUDGE
(You believe the Terror is dreadful but necessary)

"Many of these people have tried to kill supporters of the Revolution. They are murderers and deserve to die."

BUSINESSWOMAN OR MAN
(You believe the Terror is unnecessary)

"The Revolution stood for liberty and freedom so I supported it. But the Terror is destroying liberty and freedom. I'm against it"

JOURNALIST
(You believe the Terror is unnecessary)

"The Jacobins are out of control. They are using the Terror to settle their petty arguments. They just want to kill off their political opponents."

URBAN WORKER/SANS CULOTTES
(You believe the Terror is dreadful but necessary)

"The Revolution brought us cheap bread. We could afford to feed our families. But now the price of bread is rising because people are trying to make big profits. They must be stopped. They must be taught a lesson."

GOVERNMENT OFFICIAL
(You believe the Terror is dreadful but necessary)

"These are desperate times. We are still threatened by invasion. Enemies within France are even more dangerous than enemies abroad. We need desperate measures to survive."

PEASANT
(You believe the Terror is unnecessary)

"Before the Revolution we were badly treated by the nobles, now we are being badly treated by these politicians in Paris. They've ruined our churches. They've taken all our grain. The Terror is just an excuse to kick us around."

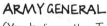

ARMY GENERAL
(You believe the Terror is unnecessary)

"The Terror is out of hand. People are being executed for ridiculous reasons. Our soldiers are risking their lives abroad to defend the Revolution. But our leaders are betraying it at home."

The Terror

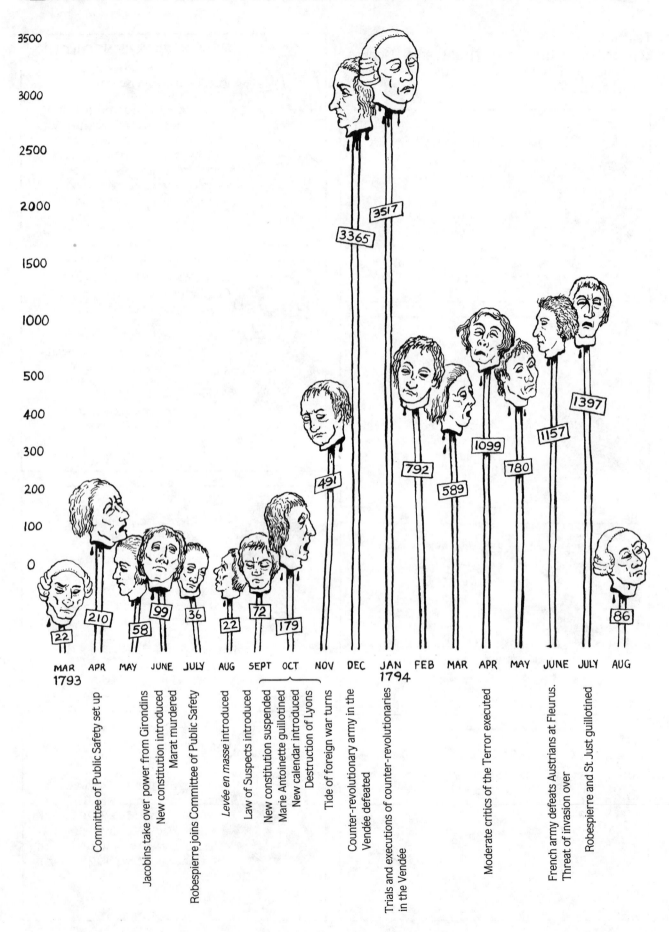

3500

3000

2500

2000

1500

1000

500
400
300

200

100

0

3517

3365

491

792

589

1099

780

1157

1397

22

210

58

99

36

22

72

179

86

| MAR 1793 | APR | MAY | JUNE | JULY | AUG | SEPT | OCT | NOV | DEC | JAN 1794 | FEB | MAR | APR | MAY | JUNE | JULY | AUG |

Committee of Public Safety set up

Jacobins take over power from Girondins
New constitution introduced
Marat murdered

Robespierre joins Committee of Public Safety

Levée en masse introduced
Law of Suspects introduced
New constitution suspended
Marie Antoinette guillotined
New calendar introduced
Destruction of Lyons
Tide of foreign war turns

Counter-revolutionary army in the Vendée defeated

Trials and executions of counter-revolutionaries in the Vendée

Moderate critics of the Terror executed

French army defeats Austrians at Fleurus.
Threat of invasion over

Robespierre and St Just guillotined

For or against the Revolution?

✸✸

THE revolutionary government could never be quite sure where its opponents were. Many opponents kept quiet, others tried to disguise their opposition. Some people secretly spread propaganda against the Revolution.

The poem on this page has been found circulating in Paris. Anyone found in possession of a copy risks being sent to jail.

Can you work out why the revolutionary government so dislikes this poem?

CLUE: FOLD THE POEM IN HALF

Loyalty I'll no longer give	to those who ruled us once
To those who rule us now	I'll ever faithful be
For in my heart I love	"The new laws": I renounce
Both King and Queen - I vow	they're no good as I can see
God's blessing alight on	all the new democrats
The noble families	can take themselves to hell
The Lord send his blight on	the old aristocrats
The elected deputies	are guardians of all that's well

The French Revolution

Look at this comic strip version of the events of
the French Revolution.
1. Write a caption for each frame.
2. Cut out the pictures and stick them onto a
   sheet of paper in the correct order.
3. Look through your book and try to put a date
   on each event.

Did Napoleon betray the Revolution?

❋❋❋❋❋❋❋❋❋❋❋❋❋❋❋❋❋❋❋❋❋❋❋❋❋❋❋❋❋❋❋❋

	THE ANCIEN REGIME	THE REVOLUTION	NAPOLEON
		*These features were suspended during the Terror	
Who rules France?	King Louis. Has absolute power. Can't be removed	No single ruler	
Is there a National Assembly?	No National Assembly has met since 1614	The National Assembly is elected by the people	
Who can vote?	No elections	All men can vote	
Who makes laws?	All laws are made by the king	All laws are made by the Assembly	
What are the laws like?	Chaotic system of laws. Some are very out of date	Some old laws are kept. Many new ones introduced	
... Prisons	People can be put in prison without being charged in court	People cannot be put in prison without being charged in court *	
... In the courts	Some people e.g. nobles have special rights in the courts	Everyone is equal in the courts	
... Censorship	Attempts are made to ban newspapers and books	There is no censorship *	
Who goes to school?	Only the privileged go to school	Education is supposed to be for everyone	
Who runs the schools?	The Church runs the schools. There are no state schools	State schools are proposed but not set up	
What are people taught?	Schools stress respect for elders, and teach mainly about religion	Schools aim to develop pupils' questioning attitudes	
Is there a state Church?	Only Catholicism is allowed	Any religion is allowed	
Who appoints the bishops?	Bishops are appointed by the king	Bishops are elected by the people	
Who pays for the Church?	Church is paid for by the peasants (from the church tax or tithe)	Church is paid for by the state	
Is the Church rich?	Church owns lots of land	Church lands are sold off	
The peasants	Peasants owe feudal dues to the nobles	Feudalism is abolished	
The nobility	Nobles are powerful. They have special privileges	Nobility is abolished	

Women in the Revolution

✣✣✣

How to play

■ Your aim is to reach the end of the Napoleonic Era alive — and with more points than anyone else. Points are given out during the game according to the instructions on the board. You start with five points.

■ Play in groups of four. Throw a dice and move the number of squares shown on the dice.

■ If you land on a 'life or death' square, read out what it says on the square and then throw the dice again. A throw of two or under means death. Three or over means life. On all other squares follow the instructions given.

■ Keep a record of your score.

START HERE :
THE ANCIEN
REGIME

Board squares:

12 — ALL — LIFE OR DEATH: ATTACK ON BASTILLE

11 — FEUDALISM IS ABOLISHED — +8

10 — THE REVOLUTION BEGINS: 1789

9 — YOUR FACTORY CLOSES DOWN: YOU LOSE YOUR JOB — -8

8 — YOU OWE LOTS OF MONEY — -2

7 — FOOD PRICES RISE — -6 — URBAN WORKER

13 — MIDDLE CLASS — WOMEN'S POLITICAL CLUBS ARE SET UP — +6

14 — WOMEN CAN INHERIT THEIR FATHER'S MONEY — +8 — MIDDLE CLASS

15 — URBAN WORKER — WOMEN BRING KING BACK TO PARIS. — +8

16 — PEASANT AND URBAN WORKER — FOOD SUPPLIES IMPROVE — +6

17 — DIVORCE MADE EASIER — +4 — ALL

18 — DECLARATION OF THE RIGHTS OF WOMEN — +10 — ALL

19 — WOMEN HELP IN THE WAR EFFORT — +2 — ALL

20 — THE TERROR BEGINS: 1793

21 — CHARLOTTE CORDAY KILLS MARAT : HER PLAN BACKFIRES — -4 — ALL

22 — NEW CONSTITUTION IS SUSPENDED — -6

1 — WOMEN ARE NOT ALLOWED TO VOTE — -4

2 — PEASANT WOMEN HAVE TO PAY FEUDAL DUES. — -10 — ALL

3 — A PROPOSAL IS MADE: ALL WOMEN WHO OWN PROPERTY SHOULD BE ALLOWED TO VOTE. — +4 — URBAN WORKER

4 — LIFE OR DEATH: BAD HARVEST — THREAT OF STARVATION

5 — GOOD MARRIAGE BRINGS YOU GREAT WEALTH — +6 — MIDDLE CLASS AND URBAN WORKERS

6 — WOMEN DISCUSS NEW IDEAS — +2 — MIDDLE CLASS

23 — LIFE OR DEATH: REVOLUTIONARY TRIBUNAL

24 — FOOD PRICES HIGH : URBAN WOMEN GO HUNGRY. — -8 — ALL

25 — EMIGRE NOBLE WOMEN PLOT AGAINST THE REVOLUTION — -8 — ALL

26 — WOMEN'S POLITICAL MEETINGS BECOME INCREASINGLY VIOLENT — -2 — ALL

27 — WOMEN ARE BANNED FROM THE PUBLIC GALLERY OF THE CONVENTION — -10 — MIDDLE CLASS

28 — WOMEN LEADERS ARE GUILLOTINED — -12 — MIDDLE CLASS

29 — WOMENS' POLITICAL CLUBS ARE CLOSED DOWN — -14 — MIDDLE CLASS

30 — THE NAPOLEONIC ERA BEGINS: 1799

31 — NAPOLEON DISCOURAGES WOMEN'S EDUCATION — -12 — ALL

32 — NAPOLEONIC CODE REDUCES WOMENS LEGAL STATUS — -10 — ALL

33 — NAPOLEON SAYS WOMEN ARE MACHINES FOR PRODUCING CHILDREN — -4 — ALL

34 — DIVORCE IS MADE MORE DIFFICULT — -6 — ALL

35 — NAPOLEON MAKES HUSBANDS HEAD OF THE FAMILY — -8 — PEASANT AND URBAN WORKER

36 — NAPOLEON BELIEVES WOMEN ARE IRRESPONSIBLE — -2

37 — WOMEN ARE NOT ALLOWED TO VOTE — -14

38 — MEMBERS OF YOUR FAMILY ARE KILLED IN THE WAR — -6

39 — LIFE OR DEATH: CHILDBIRTH

40 — 1815: CONGRATULATIONS. YOU HAVE LIVED THROUGH THE REVOLUTION AND THE NAPOLEONIC ERA. COUNT UP YOUR POINTS. HAVE YOU GOT LESS THAN YOU STARTED WITH?

102

SOCIETIES IN CHANGE THE FRENCH REVOLUTION

Napoleon's impact in Europe

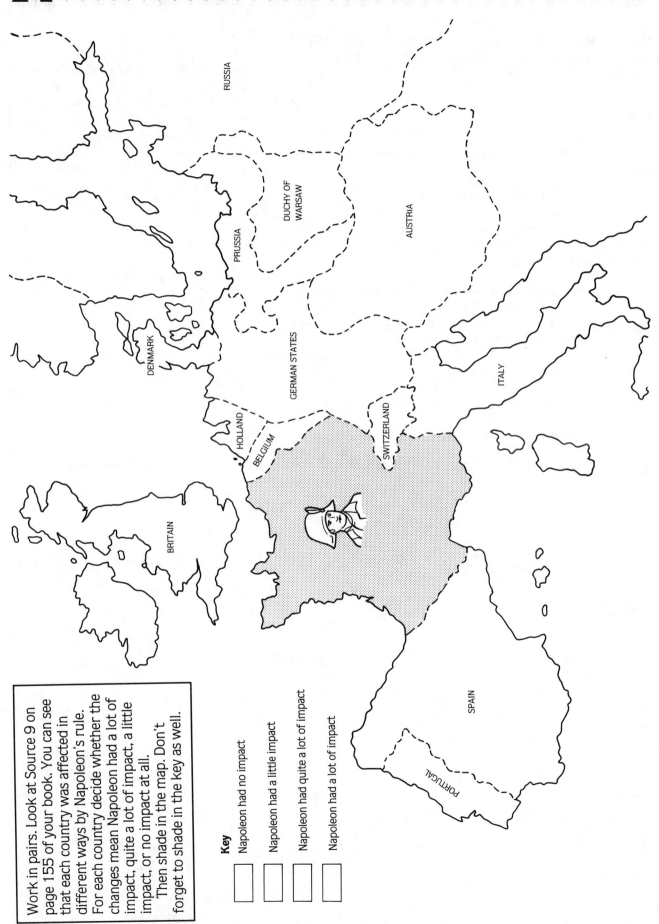

Work in pairs. Look at Source 9 on page 155 of your book. You can see that each country was affected in different ways by Napoleon's rule.

For each country decide whether the changes mean Napoleon had a lot of impact, quite a lot of impact, a little impact, or no impact at all.

Then shade in the map. Don't forget to shade in the key as well.

Key

☐ Napoleon had no impact

☐ Napoleon had a little impact

☐ Napoleon had quite a lot of impact

☐ Napoleon had a lot of impact

Cromwell and Napoleon

SOME historians have made comparisons between Oliver Cromwell – one of the leaders of the English Revolution – and Napoleon.

Look at the following statements. Decide whether the statements apply only to Cromwell, only to Napoleon or to both Cromwell and Napoleon. Mark them on the grid below and give reasons for your answer. The first one has been done for you.

	Cromwell	Napoleon
He was a very successful army officer	✓	✓
He was made ruler of his country		
He invaded other countries		
He abdicated, then tried to take over power again		
Many people thought he could sort out the problems in his country which had followed the Revolution		
He dealt with rebels very harshly		
He refused an offer to become king		
He was involved in the King's execution		

SOCIETIES IN CHANGE THE FRENCH REVOLUTION

The results of the French Revolution

✿✿✿

LOOK at the following list. Some of the items on the list are results of the French Revolution. Some of them are not:

- caused a bloody twenty-year war in Europe
- gave women the right to vote in elections
- created the revolutionary slogan 'Liberty, Equality and Fraternity', which inspired other revolutions around the world
- abolished the French monarchy
- made all French people equal in the courts
- led to the downfall of absolute monarchs throughout Europe
- created the French national anthem, the *Marseillaise*
- created the French flag – the *Tricolore*
- established a system of state education in France
- strengthened friendship between Britain and France
- introduced the guillotine as a means of execution
- gave France a written constitution
- created stronger links between countries in Europe
- destroyed feudalism forever.

1. Cross out the statements which are not results of the French Revolution.
2. From the remaining statements, select two which you think are the most important results of the French Revolution and two which are the least important. Give reasons for your choice.
3. Would your two most important results have happened without Napoleon's influence? Explain your answer.

Revolutions

✤✤

YOU have studied two revolutions – the English and the French. Now you can compare them.

Answer each of the following questions by writing a sentence or drawing a picture in the space underneath.

1. Draw two timelines showing how long the two revolutions lasted.

2. Which revolution was the more violent?

3. Who was the most important person in each revolution?

4. Which revolution was more badly needed by the ordinary people?

5. What was the best thing done in each revolution?

6. What was the most terrible thing done in each revolution?

7. Name two other changes each revolution caused.

8. Did these changes last for a long time?

9. Were there any similarities between the two revolutions?

10. Which revolution was the most important?

Discovering the Past in Key Stage 3

A form is provided below for ordering inspection copies of the following
Discovering the Past titles:

■ **Contrasts and Connections** Y7 core text and Teachers' Resource Book
  The Roman Empire
  Medieval Realms
  Islamic Civilisations

■ **Castles and Cathedrals** supplementary study unit for Y7

■ **Peace and War** Y9 core text and Teachers' Resource Book:
  Expansion, Trade and Industry
  The Era of the Second World War

■ **Britain and the Great War** supplementary study unit for Y9

Order form for **Discovering the Past** [824]
Please send me (when available):

❑ Contrasts and Connections
  ISBN 0 7195 4938 8 £7.50

❑ Contrasts and Connections
  Teachers' Resource Book
  ISBN 0 7195 4962 0 £16.95

❑ Castles and Cathedrals
  ISBN 0 7195 4952 3 £4.95

❑ Castles and Cathedrals
  Evaluation pack (Pupils' book &
  40pp Teachers' notes)
  ISBN 0 7195 4979 5 £10.50

❑ Peace and War
  ISBN 0 7195 4977 9 £7.95 prob

❑ Peace and War
  Teachers' Resource Book
  ISBN 0 7195 4978 7 £17.95 prob

❑ Britain and the Great War
  ISBN 0 7195 5148 X

❑ Britain and the Great War
  Evaluation Pack
  ISBN 0 7195 5152 8

Name...

Position...

School...

....

Postcode..

LEA...

Please return to: Judith Reinhold, John Murray, FREEPOST, London W1E 7JZ
(no stamp needed within the UK)